UNMASK THE
CONFIDENT
LEADER
WITHIN

Reclaim your identity
as an assured and
successful leader

GAVIN BRYCE

R^ethink

First published in Great Britain in 2023
by Rethink Press (www.rethinkpress.com)

© Copyright Gavin Bryce

In loving memory of my dad, George,
returned to the universe too soon.

Contents

Preface

I have been asleep for the greater part of my life – as have billions of people on this planet. I went about my daily life with my eyes open and the appearance of being awake, but on a far deeper level, I was utterly unconscious.

My wake-up call took place when I was forty. It was delivered forcefully and convincingly by Richard Wilkins and Liz Ivory, a married couple who have made it their mission to help people become conscious of who they truly are.

I first met them at an event they were hosting in a hotel conference room in Northampton, England, in late 2014. I was not a willing participant: I'd been dragged along to the event thinking it was going to be a dull affair related to my then partner's property investing network. I had my own busy consultancy business, and I had so much work that I should have been getting on with. I didn't have time to waste. Yet there was an intriguing energy in the room that captivated me.

After a few minutes of drinking in the atmosphere, I identified two cadres of people. There were those, like me, who appeared bewildered and unsure of what was about to unfold. We were easy to spot, sporting mildly worried expressions while paying far too much attention to the biscuits on offer or appearing transfixed by the contents of our cups. We were determined to avoid eye contact with the other faction in the room, who seemed high on whatever Kool-Aid this gig was selling.

If the group I belonged to were the introverts, the others were the polar opposite. This band of extroverts hugged, laughed, and smiled warmly, like the closest of friends being reunited after years of separation. Their energy was infectious, and as I took in this scene, I thought, 'This is the weirdest property networking event I have ever been to.'

Among the hundred-strong crowd, speakers Richard and Liz were like celebrities arriving at a red-carpet event. The pair were dressed to stand out, with Richard wearing a Union Jack blazer and Liz in a mono block of shocking pink. Everyone greeted the speakers loudly and affectionately as they made their way through the room to the stage.

My gang of fellow introverts and I clung to the rear of the room as if some invisible centrifugal force was pushing us back. But as I surveyed the scene before me, I had to admit that my curiosity was well and truly piqued. Whatever the pair were about to say, it was clear that many in the audience had heard them speak before. They knew what was coming, and they seemed genuinely excited for those of us who were in the dark to hear Richard and Liz for the first time.

As I took my seat close to the front of the stage, I noticed my internal negative monologue as it launched into its usual rant, reeling off the familiar self-hate speech that had been rattling around my head for my entire life. The message *du jour* went something like this: *I don't belong here. These folks are open and outgoing, and I'm an awkward freak who isn't even comfortable in my own skin. I'm fat, ugly, and depressed. I'd better not make eye contact and hope no one notices me.* As Richard took to the stage, I felt a familiar knot of sadness tighten inside me.

To say Richard is an energetic man is an understatement. His appearance alone communicates that here is someone who exudes boundless confidence, with a youthful appetite for life. When he spoke, it was with a passion that I hadn't heard before, a mixture of excitement and determination, tinged with vulnerability and emotion. It was fascinating. When Liz joined him on stage, I warmed to her instantly too, thanks to her thick Glasgow accent and liberal use of the F-bomb. Her passion matched Richard's, making the pair a powerful double act.

There were many amazing messages that day, but one thing Richard said changed my life forever. This was much more than a property networking event. Richard and Liz's talk was about the negative voice we all have in our heads. And the simple message that changed my life? Richard seemed to look straight at me as he said, 'You realise that the negative voice – the voice that beats you up and tells you that you're not good enough – you realise it is not your voice?' This revelation was like smelling salts to my consciousness.

Let me explain. Almost daily, for over thirty years, I told myself that I was worthless, that I was ugly, that I would be better off dead. Each day, when I looked in the mirror, the voice in my head would remind me of what a waste of humanity I was. Because of this internal onslaught, I hadn't felt comfortable in my skin for decades.

But surely this voice *was* my voice? After all, it was in my head. It spoke with my Glaswegian accent and tone. Only I could hear it. Believing that the negative voice in my head was *my* voice gave it more power and authority over me. When it told me I was worthless, I believed it, because it was me saying it, not some stranger. But here were Richard and Liz, telling me something that I had never considered before.

'The negative voice in your head is not you,' they told me. 'You are the silent observer, not the voice.'

Straight away, I knew it to be true. The inner negative voice had fooled me into believing that, as it was in my head and had been with me for as long as I could remember, that it must be my voice. Accepting that it was not instantly set me on the path to freedom from the daily torment my negative inner voice would subject me to.

After that life-changing day, I attended a five-day course with Richard and Liz to better understand how to wrest my life free from the negative voice that, for decades, held me back.[1] Thanks to them, I started down a path to increased consciousness, and to happiness that grows stronger, every day.

Do I still get down and feel sad? Yes. Is my negative voice still there? Yes. But the difference today is that I no longer believe the negative voice and all the lies it spouts. What's more, I am gradually getting better at choosing how I want to think and feel each day.

---

1   For information on the five-day Broadband Consciousness course, visit: www.theministryofinspiration.com

Introduction

Leading a business or team, whether you are a business owner, partner, or employee within a private, public, or not-for-profit organisation, from the smallest micro-business to the largest multi-national, presents a unique set of challenges. The daily demands on your time, energy, and resolve can seem limitless. The pressure and sense of isolation can feel overwhelming. They say it's lonely at the top for a reason.

Leaders must successfully navigate a range of unpredictable forces to steer their businesses and teams through the rough seas of change. In the era of Covid-19 and its aftermath, the ongoing war for talent, the myriad macroeconomic challenges, and an increasingly worrying geopolitical context, the leader's role is arguably getting tougher.

Facing these external challenges requires inner strength. Yet the negative voice that we all have can get in our way. This subversive internal critic can attack and undermine us on several fronts, making taking on the many challenges of leading a business harder, more stressful, less enjoyable, and less likely to produce desirable results.

The leader's inner critic can make them second guess themselves, doubt their strategies, and erode their confidence and self-belief. It can turn them into someone who sees threats and danger at every turn, instead of opportunities and reward. The inner critic is holding too many CEOs back from being the best leaders they can and is impacting their abilities to lead happy and fulfilling lives.

I started my first business in 2007, a boutique consultancy supporting global not-for-profit organisations to better show the impact of their complex social and humanitarian projects. For thirteen years, I travelled the globe, working in over thirty low- and middle-income countries, mainly in sub-Saharan Africa. I published several papers during this career, including an academic piece on a proposed new impact evaluation method. By 2020, I had added a social care business to my portfolio, which I successfully scaled and sold during the global pandemic. Along my entrepreneurial journey, I've had my share of failure, including the unfortunate collapse of two businesses. Looking back over my leadership journey, from a humble start working as a one-man consultancy, I built a portfolio that turned over seven figures and employed forty staff.

I am a solution-focused leadership coach and management consultant. In my coaching practice, I am a Group Chair with Vistage International (UK), the world's largest CEO Peer Advisory organisation, and I coach leaders and support their teams and businesses through my UK-based consultancy, Constant Progression Ltd.

As someone who has struggled with a negative inner voice for most of my life, I understand all too well the devastating impact it can have. Despite being successful in building my first business, as I surveyed all I had achieved in those early years, I felt miserable, more stressed than I had ever been in my life, and deeply depressed. My negative voice convinced me that rather than a successful business, I had built myself a prison. My inner critic beat me up daily, leading me to believe that I would never be happy and that I had no way out of the misery I had created for myself. In my darker moments, this hateful voice became so powerful it even led me to contemplate suicide.

My purpose has always been to help people, to be of service. Since selling my social care business, my focus has been on magnifying leaders' potential to create greater impact in what they do, while living more fulfilling lives. I want to take my experience of running my own businesses and my personal struggles with the inner saboteur and help others by coaching them through their issues, challenges, and opportunities.

In the years that I have been coaching and working as a management consultant, I've found that, often, the biggest challenge facing my clients is the battle going on between their ears. An internal battle that can leave impressive individuals lacking confidence in their abilities. My approach to coaching leaders starts with an exploration of their inner negative voice to understand how it may show up in their leadership and lives.

All eight billion people on our planet have (or will have) a negative voice in their heads. All of humanity has that in common. The negative voice doesn't affect everyone equally, and it can be more present at certain times in our lives than others. What's clear is that many of us will struggle with this voice at points, whether or not we realise it. And for some people, the internal war can be a relentless, daily agony.

In leadership roles, the negative voice can erode our confidence in our abilities, adding unnecessary stress and anxiety to an already complex and challenging role. It can make us feel like we don't know what we're doing, or that we're not good enough. It may compare us with other 'more successful' leaders and then beat us up for not measuring up. Perversely, the negative voice typically compares our weaknesses with other people's strengths. For some leaders, it can have an imposter-syndrome effect, making them believe they are a fraud who is going to get caught out at any moment.

If that's not bad enough, it's not just *your* negative voice you have to contend with. Every person in your organisation has also brought their inner critic to work. Left unchecked, the impact these inner saboteurs can have on you, your leadership, your teams, and your business is potentially huge. It can cause a breakdown of trust between team members, contribute to higher levels of unconstructive conflict, and may give rise to outright hostility. This in turn can lead to poor decision making, diminished productivity, and dwindling quality. In such a toxic culture, few can thrive, yielding a loss of talent and heaping more stress and anxiety onto those who remain in the business.

In the position of leader, it can be soul destroying to survey your business and witness this kind of decline, not knowing what to do to turn things around. Your business, once a source of pride and joy, can, for some, feel like an elaborate trap from which there is no escape.

This is where I come in. Having successfully quelled my negative voice and coached other senior executives through my simple process, I will show you how to reclaim your identity as a confident and successful leader.

As the ultimate decision maker, whether of your own business, or as a senior executive in the B- or C-suites, you want your leadership to make a tangible difference in the achievement of your organisation's strategic vision. You want the decisions you make to further the business's mission, while consolidating your team's efforts around a shared purpose and set of core values that attracts top talent and keeps everyone motivated. You want your customers to love your products or services so much that they become lifelong loyal fans. Put simply, you want your leadership to *matter*.

I will show you how to unmask your true leadership identity by explaining how to expose and reject the inner critic that is holding you back – in business and in life. Unlike some other books on this subject that can baffle the reader with neuroscience and complex models of human psychology, my approach is so simple you can implement it right away. If you choose to accept my straightforward system of rediscovery and practise the easy-to-apply techniques I will share with you, you'll be immediately on the path to confident leadership and a happier you. My promise to you is that, with practice, the effects of unmasking your true leadership identity will get stronger each day.

I have written the book in three parts. Part One begins our journey together by introducing you to the concept of the Mask – the name I give to the negative inner voice – and sharing my personal story. This part of the book will give you a greater understanding of how the Mask emerges and how you can expose it in your life. In Part Two, I move on to explore the impact the Mask can have on our lives and how easily it can assume our identity. Finally, in Part Three I present my three-step plan to beating the Mask – Realise, Reject, and Respond. To make the application of my plan as simple as possible, I include case studies of leaders from different sectors.

By the end of this book, you will have the knowledge you need to be the leader you want to be, free from the constant internal battle. That's good for business and good for you. What's more, you will have the tools to help your teams unmask their true potential, too.

As I explained in the Preface, Richard and Liz were important messengers for me, introducing me to the concept of the negative voice. I have been further inspired and enlightened by the writings of Eckhart Tolle, Joe Dispenza, Deepak Chopra, and countless others.[2] My view is simple: the more people who are sharing these messages, the better.

When you put the simple techniques in this book into practice, you will find a path to a happier, more fulfilling life. I can tell you from my experience that the more you practise, the stronger and more lasting

---

2   See the Further Reading section for a range of titles I have found inspiring.

the effects will be. Understanding how to expose and then reject negative thinking is the key to unlocking who you truly are as a leader. I dare you to be wrong about who you think you are.

How to use this book

To take on board the ideas I am about to present, I need a favour. As you read, I ask you to choose to accept what follows, without over-thinking it. To move out of your head and into your heart. Trust the process – this will make it easier for you to try the simple techniques I am going to share.

I assume you are reading this book because you recognise the destructive effects the negative voice can have. This might be the result of direct, personal experience, whereby your leadership and life are being held back because of a harmful inner monologue. Maybe you are witnessing its damaging effects around you, whether in your business or personal life.

You will get more from this book if you choose to accept my ideas as true. If you feel resistance as you read, stop for a moment, observe this, and ask yourself, 'Where is my resistance coming from?' Witness any resistance you experience. Once you have set it aside, come back to the book with an open heart (and mind). Take it all in and, when you have reached the end, if you wish to analyse my suggested approach, that's okay.

My aim in writing this book isn't to present a rigorous scientific model of how the brain works. My aim is to give you a simple, powerful system for living your life more consciously. This is the foundation for being a confident and successful leader. I want to help you spend more of your life being the real you.

I believe in simplicity and wanted to present ideas in an easy-to-understand way so that anyone can wrap their head around them. My experience of using this system has been life changing. I hope it will be the same for you.

Let's get started.

PART ONE
EXPOSE THE MASK

The promise of this book is to help you unmask the confident leader that lies within. In Part One, I will introduce the concept of the Mask, how it can show up in our lives and how to expose its identity. I will share with you my personal battle with the Mask and how I learned to overcome its deeply destructive impact on my ability to be a confident leader.

ONE

The Mask Within

The negative voice I talk about in this book goes by many names. I have used the 'inner critic' and the 'inner saboteur', but I have also heard it referred to as 'the ego', 'the chimp' and 'the pain-body'. My mentors, Richard and Liz, call it 'The Script'. I am sure you have heard it go by other names, too. For our purposes here, and to help bring to life my system of rediscovering your leadership identity, I will henceforth refer to the negative voice as the 'Mask'.

How can a voice be a mask? When we think of a mask, we imagine a physical object that obscures our face, our features, and our identity. When I speak of the Mask, however, I want you to think bigger than just a costume item worn on Halloween or at Venetian balls. I want you to imagine the Mask as an invisible, fictional character of your mind, who lives within you. When I write about the Mask having a voice, it is the character of the Mask that I am referring to. Keep that idea of an invisible character in mind as you read.

I want you to imagine that the Mask that lives within you has the power to offer you thoughts, feelings, and actions. Notice my use of the word 'offer'. I use it intentionally to underscore that you have a *choice* to accept or reject what your Mask offers you. The Mask will never offer you anything that you would consciously choose for yourself. Let me explain what I mean when I say 'consciously' or 'conscious'. In most situations, if I offered you the choice of feeling happy or sad, you would likely choose happiness. If I offered you the choice to be confident or unconfident, you would pick confident. Hence, if you were to feel sad or lacking in confidence, those feelings will have arisen unconsciously. You would not have been conscious because you would not have chosen to feel these ways.

This is where the Mask comes in. The Mask will always offer you thoughts, feelings, and actions that you would not consciously choose, ones that you don't like and don't want. As we shall learn, the Mask only knows fear, so every thought, feeling, or action that it suggests is based entirely on fear.

It is up to you whether you accept what the Mask offers you. As we shall discover in later chapters, if you do not consciously choose what to think or how to feel and act, the Mask will choose for you. In this way, the Mask has the power to project itself onto your identity and assume control. This ability to manifest itself externally, superimposing itself on your identity, is where the Mask gets its name.

While the Mask helps us to understand why we may think, feel, and act in ways that are contrary to what we would consciously choose, it is not a get-out-of-jail-free card. Knowing about the Mask helps us to understand our negative thoughts, feelings, and actions, but it does not excuse them. For if the Mask is in control, it is because we have allowed it to be.

Imagine for a moment you find yourself in an argument with a loved one. As the argument intensifies, your Mask offers you anger. As you unconsciously accept the offer of anger and move into it, the anger shows up on your face, in your voice, and in your posture. In this moment, the Mask transforms from an invisible character that lies within to an external projection that hides your true identity.

Importantly, we can take the Mask off and reveal our true self underneath. But what if we don't realise we are wearing it? What if we have been wearing it for so long that when we look in the mirror, we see the character of the Mask as our identity? What if, over time, we forget our true identity that has been there all along, under the shadow of the Mask?

The four cornerstones of the Mask

The concept of the Mask rests on four cornerstones:

1. **We all have a Mask.** This is the first idea I ask you to accept: that we all have an inner negative voice, which I call the Mask.

2. **We are not the Mask.** You – the real, conscious you – are not the Mask.

3. **The Mask is a fictional character** of the mind that represents any thoughts, feelings, or actions that we wouldn't consciously choose.

4. **We cannot get rid of our Mask.** While we can learn to minimise and beat the Mask, we can never lose it entirely.

Let me bring this to life. Would you choose to have hateful thoughts about yourself? Would you choose to feel worthless? Would you choose to shout angrily and hurtfully at someone you love and respect over a trivial argument? If you wouldn't choose these things, yet you are having hateful thoughts, feeling worthless, and acting in ways that needlessly hurt people you love, who is choosing to do that? Who is in control?

We are all born without a Mask. As newborns, we are completely vulnerable to the world we are delivered into, reliant entirely on the adults in our lives to pro-tect and nurture us, whomever they may be. As our senses develop, we begin to understand and interpret the world. As part of this, we recognise potential danger in our environment. We learn not to touch dangerous things, such as hot cookers, fires, and sharp knives, for example.

As our communication skills develop, we learn the rules of our social surroundings, such as not to run in the corridor at school, that we must finish our meal before we can leave the table at home, to always say 'please' and 'thank you', and to pay attention to the teacher when in class. We learn these rules from those around us – our parents, siblings, aunts and uncles, grandparents, neighbours, friends, and teachers. We also learn from other sources of information in our environment, such as social media, the internet, television, music, books, and mass advertising.

Importantly, our young minds are constantly soaking up all the information around us like a sponge. If we are in the same room as our parents and they are having a conversation that doesn't involve us, we are still absorbing and processing that information. That goes for any context and any situation – young minds are never 'off'; they are continuously receiving and interpreting information.

The brain comprises many parts, some older than others from an evolutionary perspective. The oldest parts of our brain are collectively called the limbic system and are found in the centre of the brain, with the newest part, called the neocortex, found on the surface.

The limbic system is involved in our emotional and behavioural reactions, particularly those crucial to our survival response, while the neocortex is involved in higher-level thinking and handles cognition and consciousness.[3] I promised to keep things simple, so that's the end of the biology lesson. If you would like to learn more about how the brain works and its different functions, I would recommend *A Thousand Brains* by Jeff Hawkins for an insightful and scientifically up to date overview of the field of neuroscience.

Why do we have a Mask?

If the fictional character of the Mask 'lives' anywhere, it is in our old brain, as it relates to our survival responses. I like to refer to the human survival mechanism as the 'Triple-F' system. In response to threat, we will typically do one of three things:

1. Fight: Get ready to attack or be attacked, moving towards danger

2. Flight: Get ready to run away from danger

3. Freeze: Stay perfectly still, say nothing, and perhaps the danger will move on and leave us alone[4]

---

3   J Hawkins, *A Thousand Brains: A new theory of intelligence* (Basic Books, 2021)

4   M Taylor, 'What does fight, flight, freeze, fawn mean?' (WebMD, 28 April 2022), www.webmd.com/mental-health/what-does-fight-flight-freeze-fawn-mean, accessed May 2023

To be clear, the Triple-F system *is* important to our survival. Our early human ancestors would have relied heavily upon this safety system to protect them from the various dangers present in their hunter-gatherer lifestyle and environment. While we no longer need to hunt dangerous prey for our next meal, we have other physical dangers in our environment that mean we still rely on the Triple-F system. For example, I was crossing the road recently with my dog and halfway across, a small van that hadn't seen me turned aggressively into the road at speed, with me and my dog in its path. My flight response activated in a split second and I leaped out of the way of the oncoming vehicle. Upon safely reaching the other side of the road, my blood was coursing with adrenaline and I was feeling the various aftereffects of almost dying: shock, then relief, and then anger at the careless driver who'd almost killed me and my dog.

Importantly, we do not have to consciously activate our survival mechanism. In my example above of the oncoming van, if I'd had to think about what to do, the seconds it would have taken to decide on a course of action could have been the difference between life and death. I didn't need to think about it at all – that's what makes this system so effective at keeping us alive.

While our physical environment now is less dangerous than that faced by our early human ancestors, our Triple-F protection system still does an amazing job of keeping us safe from physical harm and death, most of the time. But there's a problem. In our modern, inter-connected, and technologically advanced societies, the limbic brain struggles to distinguish between real physical danger, such as almost being hit by a vehicle, and a perceived threat, such as receiving an angry, but innocuous email from a colleague.[5] This is where the Triple-F system can work against us, perceiving danger and risk where none is present.

On a conscious level, we recognise that an email from an aggrieved colleague, while annoying, is not a physical threat to our survival. The problem is that the limbic system cannot distinguish this important difference, triggering the Triple-F response and bombarding your body with all the hormones necessary to fight, take flight, or freeze. Without your conscious recognition of the absence of genuine danger, your limbic system may respond to your colleague's angry email as if it were life-threatening. What happens next is where it gets interesting.

The microsecond between the Triple-F system being triggered and your response to the perceived danger is the space where the Mask exists. Let's expand upon the example of receiving a rather unprofessional and negative email from a colleague. You open the email, completely unguarded, not expecting any issue or problem. The email is from Jim, a colleague in your

---

5   R Kalhorn, 'What to do when stress puts you in "survival mode"' (INSEAD Knowledge, 15 September 2020), https://knowledge.insead.edu/leadership-organisations/what-do-when-stress-puts-you-survival-mode, accessed April 2023

sales team and one of your direct reports. The email starts off innocently enough but as you read on, Jim's tone becomes more frustrated, angry even. He blames you for changing the sales targets and believes it's your fault he won't get his bonus this month. He threatens to take the matter to HR and lets you know he is thinking about making a formal grievance.

Without you making a decision, your Triple-F system springs into action and your body is awash with all the chemicals it needs to fight, flight, or freeze. As part of this subconscious process, your Mask will offer you thoughts, feelings, and actions. Let's look at three potential scenarios in this situation, where your Mask is in control.

Scenario 1: The Mask offers 'fight'

Having read the email, you angrily bang your desk, push your chair back, forcefully slamming it into the wall, and shout an expletive as you stand up and march towards Jim to confront him. When you arrive at his desk, not waiting for him to say a word, you launch into an aggressive tirade, shouting in his face, with everyone in the office watching the scene unfold. You are furious. And things are just getting started. Reacting to your confrontational approach through his own Triple-F system, Jim is now in full fight mode, too. Rising to his feet, you are inches from each other's faces, like two boxers in the ring about to start the grudge match of the decade. This isn't going to end well.

Scenario 2: The Mask offers 'flight'

You started the day feeling positive and were looking forward to getting through the various tasks on your to-do list. Today was going to be a good day. Then you got Jim's email. As you read, you take in Jim's anger and frustration, and you feel crushed. A sense of defeat and helplessness washes over you and all your earlier motivation to have a productive day drains away. You feel your mood crash and now you can't face Jim, or anyone. You switch your computer off, tell your PA that you have a headache and leave the office. When you get home, you retreat to the bedroom and pull the covers up around you. You switch your phone off, eager to be completely alone and disconnected. It's 11am on a Monday.

Scenario 3: The Mask offers 'freeze'

As you read Jim's email, you feel anxious about the consequences of HR involvement and a potentially messy grievance process. This is not the start to the week you were hoping for. You feel paralysed, with no idea what to do next. There are so many options spinning around in your head. Should you speak with Jim? Should you approach HR? Should you call a senior leadership team meeting? What a mess. Feeling utterly overwhelmed by the situation, you decide to forget about it. In fact, you decide to delete the email from Jim; that way, you won't have to think about it. Trouble is, it's *all* you can think about, and now you have the added anxiety of knowing that you are avoiding dealing with the situation. As you try to move on to complete other tasks, your brain is filling up and worrying about all the things that could go wrong. The feeling of paralysis returns. As you leave the office, you reflect on how unproductive you have been. You haven't been able to focus all day.

In the above scenarios, after the brain's automatic Triple-F system detects potential danger, the Mask takes over. I have presented three distinct scenarios, but in real life, a combination is more likely. You may start with thoughts and feelings that prompt you to fight, which then give way to feelings of flight, for example.

The easiest way to identify that your Mask is in control is to ask this simple question: would I choose to think, feel, or act this way? If the answer is 'no', your Mask is in control and making those choices for you.

The Mask has the power to govern your life, without you even knowing it. Like an actor in a movie, you play the part the Mask has written for you. We accept when we watch a movie that the actor and the character they play are separate identities. As convincing as Daniel Craig may be as the fictional British spy 007, we accept he is not actually James Bond, with a licence to kill. Craig and Bond are two different identities. This becomes apparent when we see the same actor in a different role. Think about how different James

Bond is from Daniel Craig's character Benoit Blanc in the *Knives Out* movie series.

When in character, the actor is wearing a mask. The mask worn by the actor to play a particular role will determine how they think, feel, and behave. The mask will dictate their personality, their hairstyle, and what they wear. It will direct their interactions with people, what they say – and don't say – and what actions they take in different situations. When we watch a movie, we accept that, no matter how real it may feel, the actor is not the character they're playing.

Yet, in life, we too are wearing a mask, unconsciously playing a character. Our Mask tells us how to think, feel, and act in different situations. Whether we play the part the Mask has prepared for us, or choose to ignore it, comes down to how conscious we are in our everyday life. As we shall learn next, how the Mask tells us to think, feel, and act is the result of the context in which we grew up. Created from your environment as you develop as a child, large parts of the programming for your Mask come directly from those you grew up around, including your parents, siblings, extended family, even friends. Each of us has a unique Mask and the single biggest clue as to who our own Mask is telling us to be, is to recognise the Masks of those who raised us. To illustrate this idea, the next chapter presents a personal account of the emergence of my Mask.

Summary

This chapter has introduced the 'Mask', a fictional character of the mind responsible for the thoughts, feelings, and actions that we would not consciously choose or want for ourselves. We all have a Mask, an inner negative voice, yet we – our true, conscious selves – are not our Mask. We are not our negative thoughts.

Our Mask is a product of our evolution, linked to our primitive brain's survival response, which I have called the Triple-F system. Because our Mask is hardwired into our brain's survival response, we cannot get rid of it entirely. This system offers us three possible responses to a threat or danger: fight, flight, or freeze. Our Mask is continuously surveying our environment, looking for potential threats and danger. How our Mask responds to perceived threats and danger is influenced by our context growing up, particularly those we live with.

The Mask acts at the subconscious level; if we do not consciously choose our thoughts, feelings, and actions, our Mask will choose for us. In this way, the Mask has the power to assume our identity. As the Mask's choices will never be those we would consciously make for ourselves, the impact on us and those around us can be damaging.

TWO

A Mask Is Born

He died at home, in the loving company of his wife, Jackie and daughter, Claire. I was absent as my dad drew his last breath and left us forever. He had been unconscious for days, in an unchanged state, and the constant bedside vigil meant we were short on food and other supplies. I had volunteered to go to the supermarket to get essentials. It was a quick errand, but the respite it offered was welcome after days spent at my parents' house, watching the man we all loved slowly fade away.

Having defeated sarcoma, a rare form of cancer, just a year earlier, the disease came knocking again in early 2019, this time as mesothelioma – another rare form, linked to asbestos exposure. My dad had been a welder on the River Clyde since he was sixteen, working inside the large asbestos-lined engines that would power the ships that made the river famous. Working inside those engines as a young man and seeing the asbestos hang in the air like thick snow, my dad had recalled that as the particles fell from the air and stuck to the men's hair, skin, and clothing, it covered them completely until they looked like 'white mice'. As he worked, my dad and thousands of other men like him breathed the toxic material deep into their lungs, leaving a silent ticking time bomb that, after a fifty-six-year countdown, had now detonated.

Despite knowing this cancer to be terminal, my dad took every treatment the medics offered him to extend the time he had left, often at the expense of his quality of life. At diagnosis, his consultant had given him a maximum of twenty-four months to live, and my dad wanted every single one of them. In his mind, he had set a target.

In the first year, he put himself through round after round of chemotherapy in the hope it would give him the best chance of being around for as long as possible. Long enough to celebrate his fiftieth wedding anniversary with the love of his life; more time to watch his grandchildren, Lucas and Lara, grow up; and extra, precious days to enjoy the company of his children.

If 2019 was the year of fighting his cancer, 2020 was the year of acceptance and steady decline. We began the year with a celebration of Dad's life, a party held on his seventy-third birthday and attended by his six brothers, their wives and children, relatives from my mother's side of the family, friends aplenty, and even comrades from his brief time in the Paratroopers. It was a perfect evening, filled with so much love and joy it almost suppressed the deeply sad reason that had brought us together. Almost.

My dad's sheer strength of will and the unwavering support of my mother got him so close to his target. By July 2020, time had run out, and we prepared to provide end-of-life care for him at home. The bitter-sweet morphine injections that would ease his pain and suffering, which as a family we of course wanted, began. Yet, the administration of this strong opioid signalled the end and, despite months of preparing for the worst, none of us was ready to say goodbye.

We spent the last few days around his bed, sharing stories. He didn't say much but we could tell he was listening and enjoying our company. My mum barely let go of his hand. We watched episodes of *Still Game* together, a BBC Scotland comedy that is soaked in Glaswegian cultural references and humour. He even enjoyed a small glass of wine. It felt familiar and warm. Then he fell asleep and into unconsciousness. We remained by his bedside for three more days.

The fact that he emigrated to the universe while I was in Asda is entirely consistent with his dark,

Glasgow-born humour. Returning from my brief shopping trip, I pulled the car into the quiet, cottage-lined street where my parents lived. As I scanned for a parking space, I noticed a nurse leaving my parents' home. This was not unusual, nurses and care staff had been coming and going for days now, but something in the way she held her head, bowed low and sombre, made my stomach ache.

As I walked through the front door, shopping bags in hand, the sense of grief hit me instantly. The cries of my mother and sister from the kitchen told me he had died. I walked numbly into the house to be met with an emotional scene of mother and daughter comforting one another. I placed the shopping on the floor, waiting for the words I knew were coming. 'He's gone, Gavin. He stopped breathing just a few moments ago.' I gave my mum and sister a hug, absorbing their grief like a sponge. My mum motioned towards the bedroom where my dad had lain unconscious for several days. 'Go and see him,' she said, urging me towards the closed door. As I walked into the bedroom, the first thing I noticed was his colour. This was only the second time I had seen a dead body, the first being my dad's mother, who had died decades earlier. To me, his skin looked almost cream-like, devoid of any tinge of life now that his heart had stopped pumping.

My relationship with my dad had been a complex one. We had grown much closer in later life, yet the dad

I knew in my formative years was someone I feared rather than loved. The tension and distance between us grew as I reached my early twenties, only showing signs of subsiding in my thirties.

My dad had a powerful Mask, and it kept its grip on him until the end. His Mask found it hard to express love. It was aggressive, often making my dad inaccessible to those he loved most. Even at the end of his life, I believe my dad's Mask prevented him from saying what he truly felt. His Mask wouldn't let him show vulnerability, even as he faced death.

In the months before he died, my parents and I toured the Highlands of Scotland in my motorhome. We visited some of the most beautiful places, including the Isle of Skye and John O'Groats, steeped in memories for us all. I had intended to ask my dad to tell us his story one evening during the trip and, on our third night, in the stunning setting of Gareloch, I got my chance. The three of us sat around the motorhome's lounge table and poured some wine to help the words and memories flow.

My dad began with his earliest memory. The second eldest of seven brothers, my dad's early years seemed to lack the boundless, demonstrative love that young children need to feel safe. His father was ruthlessly violent, dishing out punishment on his children for the mildest of misdemeanours, often with the use of a leather belt.

His upbringing in Glasgow in the '50s and '60s was at the height of a wave of violent knife crime in the city.[6] Gangs ruled the working-class housing estates where he lived. As my father spoke, I thought about how hard it must have been to be a kid in such an environment. To live carefree seemed impossible. As a child, he must have felt like the threat of violence and danger was all around him.

When he turned sixteen, my dad escaped this life by becoming an apprentice welder in the shipbuilding yards that lined the River Clyde in those days. Yet here too he had to project a tough façade, as the yards were filled with hard men, doing even harder work. Any sign of weakness would have been like blood in the water, attracting the unwanted attention of aggressive types who thrived in this testosterone-fuelled environment.

As he told his story, my dad laid bare the origins of his Mask. I believed my father to be a sensitive, deep man. Unfortunately for him, the world he was born into had required him to be tough and bury any signs of weakness, and that's what his Mask did. His Mask was gruff, abrasive, guarded, aggressive, and emotionally closed off. In the shipyards of Glasgow, his Mask identity enabled him to blend in seamlessly with all the other men's Masks, keeping unwanted attention at bay.

---

6   'The Aftermath: the "Razor Gangs" legacy', *Crime and Investigation* (no date), www.crimeandinvestigation.co.uk/crime-files/glasgow-gangs/aftermath, accessed April 2023

In his personal life, though, my dad's Mask was ineffective and destructive. At home, he had a loving wife, a young son, and a baby daughter who posed no threat to him at all. If only he had learned about his Mask back then, he would have realised that he was not the person it made him believe he was. I wish he could have realised that the Mask was an identity he didn't have to own. If he had, he could have shown and received love unguardedly, been free to be vulnerable, to express his love.

My dad's difficult upbringing and ownership of his Mask identity made him hard. Even in the face of death, his Mask was firmly in charge. We all tried to break through – my mum, my sister, and me. Sometimes his light shone brightly. I recall a weekend I spent with him learning the basics of motor boating. In the group environment, he seemed so natural and funny, making jokes, often at the instructor's expense. These occasions were too infrequent, sadly, and I regret deeply that I could not help my dad recognise that he had a Mask and learn how to reject it.

I stood beside him in death and looked down at his face. I kissed his still-warm forehead and told him I loved him. As complex as our relationship had been, I had thought that I had let go of all my anger and frustration towards him. We'd had so many positive, soul-searching conversations in recent years. Yet, alone with my dad in that moment, I felt a massive weight lift off me. Years of suppressed anger, rage, and disappointment seeped out of me and disappeared. In death, all is stripped away, including everything that is not you. I was seeing my dad without his Mask for the first time. It enabled me to let all that suppressed emotion dissolve, and in an instant, it was gone forever.

As I turned to leave the room, I looked back and questioned whether I had ever really known my dad. I still ask myself this question today. Over the years, I had seen glimpses of his wicked humour and easy-going nature. I had seen him be vulnerable for the briefest of moments and tell me some of his story. I witnessed his tenderness towards my mum and the love he felt for his family. Yet these moments were, for me, sadly all too brief.

My dad's powerful Mask had a profoundly deep impact on me growing up. He unknowingly handed me parts of it, especially those parts that helped him to survive in a tough place. My dad had inherited parts of his Mask from his own father and, as my Mask developed in my early years, it already knew how to be aggressive and how to close off my emotions to the world around me.

The Mask takes over

I was born in Glasgow, a city still in the chokehold grip of sectarianism. I was born a Christian Protestant. The prevailing social norm when I was growing up in the 1970s dictated that I must support the Rangers football team. Had I been born Catholic, I would have been expected to support Celtic. Any deviation from this norm was met with distrust, even contempt or violence. It's much the same today. Religion also dictated which school I went to (there were schools for Catholics and schools for everyone else), what activities I would get involved in after school, and who my friends would be – mostly other Protestants.

To be clear, I am not a religious person; I don't practise any religion. For the record, I also find football intensely boring. But the fact I had been born Protestant in Glasgow gave rise to a series of choices and decisions that I played no part in making. Whether or not I liked it, this became part of my Mask – an identity that I didn't want and I wouldn't choose. By the time I started school at age five, I had a Mask that told me because I was Protestant, I must dislike Catholics. That Catholics go to different schools, get taught different things, support a different football team – and I shouldn't be friends with them.

Religion is just one example of the many possible aspects of your Mask. Another is gender, depending on which the Mask will dictate how you should act, how you should look, what you should enjoy – even what careers you can and can't pursue.

Remember, the Mask represents everything you wouldn't consciously choose. If you have consciously chosen to think, feel, or act in a certain way, this represents your true identity, your conscious self. In my example, I didn't like football or religion as a child. Yet because of my context, my Mask decided for me that I should support Rangers and despise Celtic and all their supporters, and that I must not be friends with Catholics. Why, at this early stage of my development, did my Mask make these choices for me? Given the Mask's role in our survival response, it is conditioned to be fearful. From my Mask's perspective, the adoption of the prevailing cultural, social, and religious norms of my context, was necessary to my survival. These choices made by my Mask would ensure I blended in, belonged, and wouldn't be singled out for special attention. My Mask was fearful of rejection. At such a young age, I didn't know any better. Indeed, I thought *I* was making those choices – but on a deeper level, I was conflicted.

Most of my early childhood memories are of me and my mum. Her love was demonstrative, and I received lots of cuddles and kisses as a kid. Heck, I still get lots of cuddles and kisses now. We spent a lot of time together as I was growing up; she was a constant presence in my life, which made me feel secure and loved.

Memories of my dad are patchy when I was very young. He worked as a welder on the Clyde, supporting the construction of ships and oil rigs. The hours were punishing and the work often took him far from home. Unlike my mum, my dad found it hard to show love. It felt like he didn't know how to be around me as a child. I picked up on this and mirrored his awkwardness when in his presence, unsure how to act around him. My Mask was carefully scoping for potential danger.

I was born in Glasgow's East End, but by the time I was two we had moved to Partick in the west of the city. We lived on the second floor of a traditional red sandstone tenement, in a one-bedroom apartment on the busy Dumbarton Road. In my mind, this was a massive home, with a long, narrow bathroom and large living room adorned with ornate cornicing. I remember that the L-shaped hallway was great for playing with my toy cars and Evel Knievel motorbike.

To my parents, our small home was probably cramped, given that they slept in a small annex off the kitchen, just big enough to fit a double bed, giving me the only bedroom. Funny how it's only now, as I write these words, that I see my parents' sacrifice. There was no central heating, with the only warmth coming from a bottled-gas fire in the hallway and a traditional electric bar fire in the living room. Double glazing was not yet popular nor affordable. It was a cold house.

Around the age of eight, I swapped places with my parents and moved into the kitchen annex. The imminent birth of my baby sister was the reason for the switch. My only source of privacy was a curtain that I could draw to enclose myself in my world.

I loved school. I attended Dowanhill Primary School, a ten-minute walk from my home in Partick. I could be a shy kid in certain situations, but at school I was chatty, outgoing, and probably a tad mischievous. I had my fair share of the strap from the teacher for chatting when I shouldn't have been, or giggling too loudly when I should have been working. Overall, the odd misdemeanour aside, I was smart, engaged, and an excellent student.

Smacking, slapping, and spanking by teachers and parents – indeed any adult – was a culturally accepted form of punishment for children in Glasgow in the 1970s. In the home environment, when I had been naughty, I would receive, as we say in Scotland, a 'skelpt arse', meaning vigorous slaps to the backside. Whether or not your pants were pulled down to increase the pain of the 'skelp' seemed to depend on the severity of the misdemeanour. So here I was, a young kid in an environment where violence, or the threat of violence, was being used to ensure that I did as I was told. I took this lesson in, as did my Mask. I learned that breaking rules could lead to physical harm.

I spent most time at home with my mum, with dad returning later in the evenings, after work. I always felt safe in my mum's company, although even she would sometimes resort to spanking me if I misbehaved. Let me stress again that this was the '70s in Glasgow and spanking children was the prevailing social norm. I don't want you to think that my parents physically abused me growing up – that wasn't the case. But I have to acknowledge how the threat of physical harm that I experienced as a child influenced aspects of my early development and my Mask.

On the rare occasions when I would get into trouble, my mum's punishment felt balanced. It probably ended up hurting her more than me. Her momentary loss of temper – the result of her Mask being in control – faded to almost instant regret as she witnessed her child in tears. I recall how she would then soften – the result of my mum's conscious decision, not her Mask – and comfort me. She would always apologise for shouting at me or spanking me, then calmly and rationally explain why I had got into trouble, while giving me lots of cuddles and kisses. In my Mask's assessment of my home environment, it did not see my mum as a threat. Punishment from my dad, on the few occasions when it occurred, was entirely different and my Mask categorised him as a threat quite early in my development.

I recall being in the kitchen with my mum one day when my dad arrived home. He came into the kitchen and under his arm, he had a gift for me. It was a bright red radio-controlled car, the height of toy innovation in the '70s. I was obsessed with cars. I must have had at least three full boxes of toy cars, which I played with constantly. You can imagine my excitement at this shiny vehicle that moved on its own via a hand-held controller. I was overjoyed.

I don't recall all the details of what happened next, but what I do remember is that my dad wanted to play with the car first. Perhaps his intention was to understand how the controller worked so that he could teach me how to manoeuvre the car. Whatever the reason, I was an overexcited six-year-old about to be given an amazing new toy. I just wanted to get my hands on it. Instead, I had to stand impatiently by while my dad played with my new toy.

I guess my pleadings to be given the controller triggered my dad on some level. In an aggressive rage, he turned on me and spanked me. He then picked up the shiny red car and threw it violently against the kitchen wall, smashing it into a million pieces. I was confused and inconsolable, crying as he stormed out of the house, leaving my mother to literally pick up the pieces.

My dad's violent explosions of aggression left an indelible mark on me. My radio-controlled car wasn't the only victim of his temper. I had a tiny black and white TV, combined with a radio, that you could carry around with a handle. It was about the size of a toaster, and I loved it. My dad destroyed it after an argument with my mum one day and I was left, once again, confused about what had happened. What had I done wrong?

One evening, I was woken by loud voices, a thunderous bang and shattering of glass. I went to investigate what was happening. It turned out that my dad, in another fit of rage, had slammed the bathroom door so ferociously that the glass panel, which comprised around half of the door, smashed. Glass littered the hallway, and I was ushered, confused and terrified, back into my room.

On the occasions when my dad would spank me, I recall them being violent episodes. The punishment was so extreme that, after it was all over, I struggled to breathe. Looking back, I guess what I was experiencing were panic attacks, a result of the shock of being so aggressively attacked. Seeing the state I was in, my dad would then try to calm me down, but he was the last person I wanted anywhere near me. Unlike when my mother spanked me, there was no sense of balance. The punishment, when it came, was violent, terrifying, and left me shocked and traumatised.

As I recall these memories, I want to be fair and balanced towards my parents. The examples I have given were indeed traumatic for me as a child, but they were not the norm. Most of my upbringing was happy. I think my mum knew that I was becoming fearful of my father in my early years. She would often tell me that when I was sleeping at night, my dad would come into my room, kiss me good night and tell me he loved me. She wanted me to know this because she could sense that I didn't believe he loved me; she also knew that my dad found it hard to express his feelings.

Although he did love me and invested lots of time with me at weekends, taking me on fishing trips into the Scottish Highlands, I didn't know how to be comfortable in my dad's company. My Mask caused me to see him as a threat, which led to me being very guarded around him, and so our relationship was uneasy.

The Mask is all about fear

It is important to make a clear distinction between the thoughts, feelings, and actions that you would consciously choose and those offered to you by the Mask. The easiest way to achieve this is to accept that anything the Mask offers you is based on fear. We would not consciously choose fear. Let me explain.

There is a difference between experiencing fear in the now and psychological fear, which is fear of an imagined future.[7]

The reason most of us don't stand close to the edge of a high cliff is not based on fear, it is based on an understanding that to do so could result in us going over the edge and falling to our deaths. Fear is not necessary for us to avoid life-threatening situations; we can instead use our knowledge and common sense. If I were to take you to the edge of a high cliff and threaten to push you off, that would create real

---

7   E Tolle, *The Power of Now* (New World Library, 2000)

fear, experienced in the now, because your existence would be being threatened.

The Mask doesn't operate at the level of 'real' fear. The kind of fear the Mask responds to is psychological fear, which is totally imagined, completely disconnected from any immediate danger or threat to your life. In my high cliff example, the Mask will project you to the future and get you to worry about a possible scenario in which you could be pushed off the cliff. This creates feelings of worry and anxiety, based on the psychological fear of an imagined future event, something that hasn't happened, isn't happening, and might never happen. Would you consciously choose to think and feel this way? I hope not.

Summary

The Masks of those around us, including our parents, can have a significant impact on how our own Masks perceive threats and danger in our environments. There is a 'handing down' of Mask-thinking from parent to child, as we saw in my story. My Mask adopted similar defence responses to perceived danger as my dad's Mask did, including aggression and anger.

Additional factors in our environment that influence the birth of our Masks include other family members, friends, and members of our communities, our socioeconomic background, our gender, access to information, the media, and the internet, for example. These factors, to varying degrees, contribute to programming our Mask as it assesses perceived dangers and threats. By sharing the story of my early development and the environment I grew up in, I have shown how my own Mask was born.

The Mask is driven by fear. The Mask doesn't operate in the present moment; it is usually preoccupied with the past or fearful of the future. The Mask uses psychological fear to make us worry and feel anxious about situations that have not happened and might never happen.

THREE

The Emergence Of The Mask

It was during my first year at primary school that I first understood I was different. Playtime was always great fun, and there were so many enjoyable games that we played, often in large groups. One of these was 'kiss the girls and run away'. This game, concocted by the boys, involved a group of boys running up to an unaware girl and kissing her on the cheek, then running away to repeat the process with another unsuspecting girl.

While I found this game highly entertaining, I recognised that I would rather kiss the boys. Over the next few years, and certainly by the time I had reached seven years old, I came to the realisation that I was gay, and hence different from the other boys. This troubled me deeply. At that young age, I did not know what being gay meant, other than recognising that I was attracted to boys in the same way that other boys were attracted to girls. But I was sensitive and clever enough to know that the way I felt was 'wrong' – not wrong because I felt wrong, wrong because everything around me told me it was wrong.

If I was watching TV with my mum and dad, should any gay character appear or reference be made, it was clear by the way my parents reacted that this 'gay thing' was a problem. Then there was the media. It was 1981 and a new pop group called Culture Club, fronted by the flamboyant Boy George, began grabbing headlines for all the wrong reasons. The media was obsessed by Boy George's appearance, describing his choice of 'feminine' clothing and wearing of makeup as 'gender-bending'. I didn't know back then if Boy George was gay, but it was clear he was being attacked for being different. The spotlight of hate that was put on him – and others like him – for not measuring up to society's idea of what a man 'should' be, attracted vitriol at a society level.

In the same year, the AIDS pandemic exploded. Those old enough to remember how the spread of HIV/AIDS was covered in the media in the early 80s will recall it being notably fear-invoking. The message I received back then was that this was a gay disease. Some commentators in the media even went as far to say that AIDS was God's punishment for being gay, and this echoed in the surrounding communities.

I can't put my finger on exactly where or when the notion that God hates gays entered my consciousness. Had a minister from my Sunday School mentioned it? My friends at school or at the Boys Brigade? Did I pick it up from my parents or family friends? Was it on TV? Who knows, maybe it was all these things. But when this message – that God hates gay people, people like me – trickled like a poison into my consciousness, I had nowhere to turn. It felt like I had no future.

Everything around me was telling me that anyone who was gay was 'wrong' and hated by everyone, including God. Which must mean that I was wrong. To emphasise: at seven years old, I felt that I, as a human being, was wrong. I felt like a waste of humanity. That I was not a 'real' boy and so could never become a 'real' man. That if people were to find out the awful truth about me, they would hate me, reject me, possibly even harm me. The world I had been born into increasingly felt unsafe for me.

It was around this time that my Mask took control of my identity. It would speak to me gently in those early years (later, it become more hateful and aggressive), a friendly internal voice that seemed to want to keep me safe. I thought the voice in my head was just my own voice, that this was an internal conversation with myself as I tried to understand the world around me. But the voice I was listening to was not my voice; it was the voice of my Mask. Since birth, my Mask had been observing the world around me scanning for threats and danger. By age seven, it had reached the simple, horrifying conclusion that my environment was no longer safe for me.

It would whisper to me, pretending to be me, assuming my identity. It appealed to my sense of logic, as it rationalised what action I must take to protect myself from the threat of harm. In doing so, it fed on my sense of failure at being a 'real' boy, using it to build its case and weaken my resolve. It had me convinced that I wasn't like the other boys, who all liked football and 'manly' things. I didn't like to fight, but to be a 'real' man you had to physically defend yourself.

With the realisation that I was gay and with ample evidence of society's hatred of gay people, my Mask was ready to deliver its final verdict. It told me I had no future and that I would never be happy. It explained to me that my mum and dad wouldn't love me when they found out I was gay – they would ultimately reject me. It told me that if people found out my secret, they might attack me, and that I wouldn't have any friends. My Mask painted such a bleak picture of the future that, by the time it offered me its wicked advice, I felt no resistance. At seven years old, I accepted the Mask's suggestion that my best and only option was to kill myself.

The bathroom plot

Our small tenement apartment in Partick had a long, narrow bathroom with a large sash window at the far end. The bathroom suite was avocado – in vogue then, but an interior design disaster today. As you entered the long narrow space, the entire bathroom suite was laid out on the righthand wall. First the bath itself, then the sink, and finally the toilet, just below the window.

Having accepted my Mask's advice to end my life, I now sought the best way to achieve this. We lived on the second floor and to the back of the building, about 30 feet below, was a common area for the residents to hang their washing and for the kids to play. The plan was for me to jump from the bathroom window and land on the concrete below.

Over several weeks, I formulated the plan in my head. Then the day finally arrived for me to put it into action. My Mask wanted me to open the window, climb onto the windowsill and jump. But as the reality of dying, of not being around anymore, sank in, I thought of the pain it would cause my parents for their only son to take his own life. Mostly, though, I was just scared of dying.

Instead of abandoning the idea, my Mask encouraged me to formulate a different, more protracted plan to take my own life. Rather than leaping from the window in one efficient movement, I would break things down, step-by-step. I would begin at the entrance to the bathroom and each day take one step closer to the window. Then I would jump.

I set a day on which I would put this new plan into motion. When the day arrived, I remember opening the bathroom door, entering, and closing the door behind me, locking it securely. With my back against the door, facing the window, I placed my heels precisely flush with the door. This was to be my starting position.

To take my first step, I placed the heel of my right foot parallel with the front of my left foot. I waited a few seconds to mentally record that I had taken my first step. Then I snapped out of my suicidal trance and began getting washed and ready for school, as though nothing had happened.

On day two, I once again locked the bathroom door, rested my back flush against it and faced the window at the opposite end of the room. Today I had to take two steps. I repeated the step from day one, placing my right foot in front of my left. I waited a few seconds, then I lifted my left foot and placed it in front of my right – exactly like a tightrope walker. I even held out my arms to the side for balance. When the second step had been taken, I again paused to mentally record the significance of my progress, then got ready for school. The Mask's plan was well and truly underway.

It took around three weeks for me to reach the bathroom window – a consequence of having a very long bathroom and small, seven-year-old feet. The original plan was for me to lift the sash window, climb onto the ledge, and jump. Yet when I got there, I again felt that resistance. Something within me didn't want me to do this, but the voice of my Mask urged me on.

I didn't know it, but the resistance I felt as I stood at the bathroom window, contemplating whether I should jump, was the real me breaking through. The real me didn't want to die. The real me wouldn't choose to jump to my death. I wanted to live.

As this tension between my conscious self and my Mask grew, the Mask – ever cunning and wily – suggested a different way forward. Rather than jumping out of the window right now, I should instead lift the window open, just a little, each day. When the window was fully open, then I should jump. With a sense of reprieve, my conscious self retreated and fell silent. The Mask was back in control.

In the days that followed, I repeated the whole laborious ritual, placing my right foot at the threshold of the bathroom then moving slowly and deliberately, one foot in front of the other, until I reached the window. I then lifted the window just a fraction, about half an inch. I returned and repeated the rigmarole the next day, and the next. Finally, after almost two weeks of this agonising routine, the window was fully open. Now what? There was no easy way to break down climbing onto the window ledge into smaller steps. It needed one swift action. My Mask encouraged me by reminding me of the unbearable life that lay ahead of me. The biggest driver of all being the disappointment and shame my parents would feel, and their eventual rejection of me when they found out my secret. Remember, the Mask knows nothing but fear. My Mask feared this rejection above all else.

I stood on the toilet seat next to the window, pulled myself through the window opening and sat on the ledge, with my legs dangling over the side. I didn't dare look down at the ground below. I sat, terrified, on the window ledge of our bathroom, for I don't know how long. Eventually, I began to silently cry. The plan to kill myself had dominated months of my young life. Each day, I had taken one step closer to ending my life and then somehow managed to go to school and act like a 'normal' kid. The trauma of this is hard to comprehend.

I felt defeated. I couldn't jump. I just could not do it. Something pulled me back into the bathroom to safety. I closed the window and sat on the toilet seat with tears streaming down my face. In that awful moment, I had no one to turn to, no one to seek comfort or reassurance from. To speak with anyone about my thoughts and what I'd just attempted would require me to explain the reason I had for wanting to end my life. That was a risk the Mask couldn't take. To reveal my secret was to risk rejection, which my Mask feared more than it feared me jumping from a second-storey tenement window.

I swallowed down the pain, hurt, anger, and frustration. My Mask had to admit defeat on this occasion, but it wasted no time in hissing its poison between my ears. *You see, you're not a real man. You couldn't even kill yourself. You're pathetic.* In that moment, whatever was left of my conscious self slipped into the background and, for most of the next thirty-two years, my Mask took over my life.

A model to expose the Mask

I acknowledge that my Mask is incredibly powerful and has had a hugely damaging effect on my life for more years than I like to think about. There are many people like me who have struggled and continue to struggle with their Masks daily. There are also people whose Mask has had little impact on their lives to date, and others who have struggled with their Masks for periods in their lives, but who are mostly not aware of any negative effects.

While we all have a Mask, its potential for having a negative impact on our life and leadership varies from person to person. I have shared my story of the emergence of my Mask, but it's important to discover the stories of others to bring to life the various ways the Mask comes into our lives.

As a leadership coach, I have the privilege of meeting and supporting many leaders from different walks of life and sectors of the economy. While researching this book, I approached some of my clients and leadership colleagues to ask if they would be interested in sharing their stories of how the Mask emerged in their lives. I am grateful to those who did share, and I wish to acknowledge the vulnerability and courage this required on their behalf.

Collectively, the leaders I spoke with are responsible for over a thousand staff, with a combined turnover of more than £100 million. Their businesses range from small, single-shareholder firms with a handful of staff, to large national organisations with complex governance structures and hundreds of staff across multiple sites. Every leader I spoke to recognised the Mask in themselves and acknowledged the significant amount of time and energy that are consumed in managing the immediate impact and subsequent ripple effects the Mask has had in their organisations.

At this point, you might be wondering how we can learn to expose our Mask. How can we recognise the thoughts, feelings, and actions the Mask offers us and reveal its identity? How can we expose it so that we may learn to recognise its voice more swiftly when it speaks?

Brooke Castillo, founder of the Life Coach School and Master Certified Coach, developed a model which I find useful for exposing the Mask with my leadership coaching clients.[8] The model is based on earlier work by Dr Aaron Beck, the pioneer of Cognitive Behavioural Therapy (CBT).[9]

---

8   B Castillo, 'The Get Coached Model', The Life School Coach, https://thelifecoachschool.com/self-coaching-model-guide, accessed April 2023

9   A Beck, 'The Cognitive Triangle', The Beck Institute, https://beckinstitute.org/about/understanding-cbt, accessed April 2023

Castillo's model emphasises the relationship between our thoughts, feelings, and actions: in response to external circumstances, our thoughts produce our feelings, which generate actions. These 'circumstances' include events, situations, and facts. For example: it's raining outside; energy prices are going up; my partner is cheating on me. External circumstances are, in themselves, neither good nor bad. They are neither positive nor negative. It is the act of processing our external circumstances that directs us to consider whether something is good, bad, or of no concern.

The job of processing external circumstances happens at a subconscious level. This means our Mask is the first responder in interpreting what's going on around us. The Mask will assess the situation and, if it senses danger, will offer you its thoughts in the blink of an eye. Often this happens so quickly that your only clue the Mask is in control is the realisation that you have a negative or unpleasant feeling rising within you. Remember: we are not the Mask. We suffer at the hands of the Mask when we falsely believe it is who we are. That's why exposing the Mask's identity is an important first step in beating it. It helps us separate it from who we truly are.

To illustrate how we can expose the Mask, let's apply Castillo's model to the Mask-thinking we have seen in my story.

Exposing my Mask

In my formative years, my Mask was continually assessing everything around me, looking for danger. Here's an example of how it affected me.

Circumstances

By the early '80s, I had realised that I was gay. My Mask weighed this information against its assessment of the hostility towards gay people in working-class Glasgow, where I was raised. These were my circumstances.

Thoughts

In response to the circumstances, my Mask offered me thoughts such as: *Being gay is wrong... I am wrong... I am a waste of humanity... I'll never be a real man... My mum and dad won't love me if they find out... I'll have to leave home... If anyone finds out I'm gay, my life will be over... I should kill myself before people find out I'm gay.*

Feelings

This Mask-thinking produced feelings of shame, hopelessness about my future, and fear of anyone ever finding out my secret.

Behaviours/actions

Feeling this way caused me to turn inwards at a young age, and to keep quiet. The Mask now had me all to itself because I was too afraid to tell anyone I was gay – the Mask would never let me reveal this, for fear of rejection. In response to my feelings of hopelessness and fear about my future, and with a deep sense of shame about who I was, I put into motion a plan to take my own life.

Results

I attempted to kill myself but couldn't go through with the plan. This resulted in me feeling even more shame, this time shame at being a failure because *a real man would have jumped*. This experience accelerated my introspection and severely undermined my self-confidence.

The figure below shows how my Mask interpreted my circumstances, creating a series of thoughts, feelings, and actions that I would not have chosen for myself. Had I known this as a child, I may have had the courage to reject the Mask because I would have understood that it was not me. Whenever I felt shame, hopelessness, or fear, I would have known my Mask was in control and I could have chosen differently. Sadly, I didn't gain this knowledge until I was forty, and I regret how much pain my ignorance caused me.

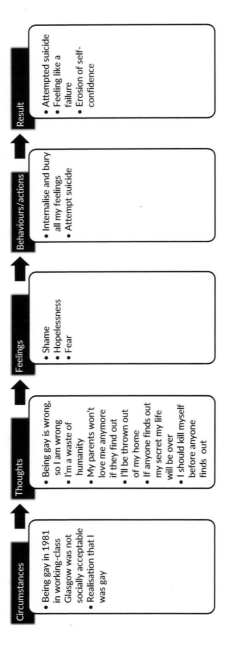

Circumstances	Thoughts	Feelings	Behaviours/actions	Result
• Being gay in 1981 in working-class Glasgow was not socially acceptable • Realisation that I was gay	• Being gay is wrong, so I am wrong • I'm a waste of humanity • My parents won't love me anymore if they find out • I'll be thrown out of my home • If anyone finds out my secret my life will be over • I should kill myself before anyone finds out	• Shame • Hopelessness • Fear	• Internalise and bury all my feelings • Attempt suicide	• Attempted suicide • Feeling like a failure • Erosion of self-confidence

Exposing My Mask

Understanding the interconnectedness of our thoughts, feelings, and actions emphasises the power Mask-thinking can have over our lives.

Being able to spot the Mask, like a suspect in an identity parade, is the first step in beating it. If you become familiar with the things your Mask typically offers you, you will be less likely to accept them and will remain under its control for less time, as you learn to spot the traces it leaves.

Summary

The emergence of the Mask is often associated with significant events in early development, typically under the age of ten. At this time, the Mask learns about 'danger' in your environment and offers you thoughts based on its fearful assessment of your context.

In this chapter, I shared with you how my Mask responded to my realisation that I was gay and its assessment of my context. My Mask led me to think that I would not be loved, that I would be rejected, that I was a waste of humanity, not a real man, and that I should kill myself. This led to feelings of isolation, fear, and a loss of hope for the future. In terms of my behaviour, I became quiet and withdrawn and I took action to end my life – all at seven years old.

I introduced Brooke Castillo's coaching model, which can be used to expose our Mask's identify by revealing its typical thoughts, feelings, and actions. Exposing the Mask is an important first step towards rejecting it as the more able we are to recognise when our Mask is in control, the sooner we can resume control and rediscover our identity.

PART TWO
REJECT THE MASK

In Part Two, my aim is to support you to reject the Mask for the fraud that it is. I will continue my story to explain why my Mask kept such a powerful grip on me for so long. Although my story is unique to me, there is nothing unique about the Mask and its preoccupation with fear. You may recognise elements of my Mask in you, or in others around you.

Then, in Chapter Five, we will examine the impact the Mask has on our leadership and life. To finish this part of the book, in Chapter Six, we will delve into how the Mask shows up in the workplace and the impact it has on culture and productivity. I hope that by seeing the Mask for the fraud that it is, including the destructive impact it has on our leadership, our lives, and those around us, it will help you to externalise the Mask and, ultimately, reject it.

FOUR

A Serious Case Of Mistaken Identity

I'd like to begin this part of the book with a reminder that *you are not the Mask*. In the coming chapter, we'll build an understanding of how the Mask robs us of our true character, as we investigate a serious case of mistaken identity.

If you have ever read any spiritual texts, particularly Buddhist ones, or if you have ever practised meditation, you may be familiar with the notion of the 'Knower'.[10] The modern-day spiritual teacher Eckhart Tolle explains this concept brilliantly in the bestseller

---

10   A Karr, 'Mahamudra: Looking directly at the Knower', *Lion's Roar* (30 June 2014), www.lionsroar.com/mahamudra-looking-directly-at-the-knower-your-guide-to-buddhist-meditationjuly-2014, accessed April 2023

The Power of Now.[11] Tolle describes the mind as a tool that we can consciously choose to use, to impressive effect. However, he suggests that, mostly, the mind uses us. To illustrate his point, he asks, 'Can you be free of your mind whenever you want to? Have you found the off button?' That most of us cannot stop thinking for more than the briefest of moments before a thought pops into our heads, suggests that we struggle to exercise control over our minds. For Tolle, this inability to stop thinking is evidence that the mind is using us.

The distinction drawn between 'you' and your mind is at the heart of understanding the Knower within all of us. The greatest delusion of our time is that we wrongly assume our mind is who we are. Consider this: if we can observe the thoughts that come into our heads, who is doing the observing? It is the observer, or Knower, that is your conscious self, which is distinct from the mind. Try the exercise below to experience the Knower within you.

EXERCISE: Experience the Knower within

Find a quiet place and sit in an upright position. Close your eyes and fall silent. Notice your breath, inhaling and exhaling deeply, slowly. Relax. Place your tongue on the roof of your mouth to relax your jaw. As the mind offers you thoughts, observe them. Do not analyse or judge them. Just observe. Feel how your presence as

---

11   E Tolle, *The Power of Now* (New World Library, 2000)

the Knower is separate from all the thoughts the mind is endlessly generating. Feel the truth that in order to observe, you must be beyond that which you are observing. You are not the mind.

The Mask is of the mind, part of the relentless chatter that seems never to stop. You, the real you, are not your thoughts. You are not your mind. You are not the Mask. You are the silent presence that observes all. You are the Knower within.

I want you to feel the power of this simple truth. Pause for a moment, close your eyes, and be still. Feel the presence within and know this to be who you truly are.

Like most of the planet, I believed that all the thoughts swirling around in my head, including those placed there by the Mask, represented who I was. For decades, I was living under this delusion, believing that the hateful torrent of self-abuse was coming from me. After decades of thinking like this, I believed it and it became who I was. We can run away from many things, including threats and danger, yet we cannot escape ourselves. But what if we are owning the wrong identity?

Understanding that we are not the Mask offers liberation. For me, this meant being able to accept that my negative thoughts were just a product of over-thinking. Knowing that all the negative thoughts and feelings belonged to the Mask and not to me, that I didn't have to believe or accept them, that I had a choice, changed my life.

If we are not our Mask, then humankind has a serious case of mistaken identity. Billions of us are walking around with our Mask firmly in control, with our true self, the Knower within, asleep and subdued. How did we get here? How has the Mask fooled so many of us for so long? Let's return to my story to understand how the Mask can insidiously take control of our identity and stay there, unnoticed, for years.

Leaving home

By the age of nine, my mum and dad moved from our small tenement flat in Partick to a larger three-bedroom semi-detached home in Glasgow's East End. My sister Claire, now a year old, was the reason for the move – we simply needed more space. I never really warmed to my new location. I had a splendid set of friends in Partick; I enjoyed school and loved living in the busy urban environment. By contrast, our new home was quiet, in a sprawling suburbia that lacked the energy I had grown used to.

While I made friends at my new school, I always felt like an outsider, like I didn't really fit in. When I moved up to high school, the problem amplified. My high school was just over two miles from my home, too far to come home for lunch. I made few real friends at school but studied hard and, despite the loneliness I experienced, I enjoyed learning.

By the early '90s, society had progressed in its views of homosexuality, becoming – thankfully – more liberal and accepting. At sixteen, I found the courage to reveal my secret for the first time, to my cousin, Lynn. I agonised over this decision, battling a barrage of Mask-thinking that terrified me into believing Lynn would tell my friends and family. The Mask wanted me to keep my mouth shut. But I had carried the weight of this truth for too long. If I was to be rejected by family, friends, and society, I needed to know. I couldn't keep living someone else's life.

Mercifully, the world didn't end when I told my cousin that I was gay. It took a while to build up to my confession and, when the words were finally out, she said, 'What, is that it? I thought you were going to tell me you were dying!' Her immediate and unwavering acceptance of my sexuality gave me courage, and for the first time in my life, I had someone I could talk to about my bottled-up emotions.

I remained cautious about who I told thereafter but felt freer with each person who knew. By nineteen, I was working in a bar and restaurant, part of a theatre that attracted a liberal-minded clientele, called the Tron, based in Glasgow's city centre. I was studying biomedical science at the University of Glasgow and, for the first time in my life, truly being myself. All my colleagues at the Tron and friends at university knew I was gay.

As part of my self-liberation, I ventured into Glasgow's gay scene and began meeting other gay men and women. It felt fantastic to see that I could be happy and loved. That I didn't need to fear rejection. I hadn't yet mustered up the courage to tell my mum and dad, but I could feel that I was getting there, and that the day was drawing close. Then, it all fell apart.

I had been out with friends at a club one Friday evening. I got a taxi just after midnight and, upon arriving home, I noticed all the house lights were on. This was unusual, as my parents would normally be sleeping. Something was wrong and I could feel my stomach tightening. As soon as I walked through the door, I could see both my parents waiting for me in the kitchen. The tension was palpable. Without waiting for me to ask what was wrong, my dad spat out the words, 'Are you gay?' I hadn't been expecting the question and the shock must have registered on my face. I'd been worried someone had died and my parents were waiting up to tell me the bad news. All I could mutter was, 'What?'

At about 9pm that evening, the phone had rung and my mum had answered. The person on the other end wasn't a friend calling for a catch-up, but a hateful individual who told my mum that I was gay and that they were going to stab me when they next saw me. Then the phone line went dead. This was 1994, before mobile phones, so there was no easy way for my parents to reach me. They'd tried calling some of my friends, but they either hadn't known where I was or didn't want to risk telling my parents for fear of outing me. Well that particular cat was now out of the bag.

We moved from the kitchen to the dining room and sat at the small table. I remember confirming that yes, I was gay, to my dad's visible disgust. For hours, my mum and dad threw a volley of questions at me. It was like they thought their interrogation could erase my sexuality, revealing that I was straight after all and this was just an elaborate hoax. They pointed out that I'd had girlfriends in the past and they wanted to understand why. Perhaps I was confused? Perhaps I hadn't met the 'right' girl yet? My mum even pleaded with me to try dating girls, just in case. It seemed never ending. My parents were confused, hurt, and just wanted to understand. I did my best to answer their naïve questions, but many of them were deeply hurtful. It was a psychologically scarring event, and my Mask was on high alert.

The onslaught continued until sunrise. We were all emotionally exhausted. There was nothing left to say and none of us had slept. Before standing up to leave the table, my interrogation over, my dad presented his closing salvo. He said, 'I accept that you are gay, but I never want to speak about it.' As if to have the last word, my mum, in complete contradiction to my dad, said, 'Well, I don't accept that you're gay and I want to talk about it.' Exhausted, I stood up from the table and numbly climbed the stairs, seeking the solitude of my bedroom. This was not how I'd envisioned coming out to my parents.

The weeks and months that followed were intense. True to his word, my dad continued life as normal as though the coming out event had never happened. My mum continued asking questions, seeking to understand what it meant to be gay, what it meant for me, and what it meant for her. At least she was trying, which felt like progress. My relationship with my dad, already on a shaky footing, had hit the rocks.

A few months of awkwardness ensued at home until emotions erupted unexpectedly one summer's day. I was in the kitchen helping my mum prepare the evening meal. I was busy peeling potatoes and chatting happily when my dad walked through the back door into the kitchen. He had a face like thunder. He turned to me, without saying hello or taking off his jacket and, in his usual aggressive tone, asked, 'This Tron place you work at' – he spat the name, as though I were in the employ of the devil – 'do you work with a girl named Anne-Marie?' I had been working at the Tron for about a year and this was the first time he had asked me anything about it. I confirmed that I knew Anne-Marie, she was the front of house manager at the theatre.

Barely allowing the words to settle in the air, he fired his next incendiary question at me: 'Does she know you're gay?' This was the first time my dad had mentioned my sexuality since the 'outing' and the question caught me off guard. In a soft, sheepish voice, I replied that everyone at the Tron knew I was gay. I thought to myself, *Why is he coming after the Tron?* It was my haven, the only place on earth where I could be myself.

Before I got the chance to ask why any of this mattered, he got to his point. You'll recall that my dad worked as a welder in the shipyards of the River Clyde. The yards were full of tough, quick-tempered men like my dad. In this environment, 'real men' didn't have gay kids. One of my dad's close colleagues, coincidently, was Anne-Marie's father. In his last words to me that day, my dad issued me with a threat. He told me I was to speak with Anne-Marie and make sure she never spoke of me or my sexuality to her father. For good measure, he added that, while I was under his roof, I would do as he said. He then left the kitchen to take up residence in his armchair in the living room.

I was in shock and lost for words. My mum had been silent during the whole encounter, and I don't recall if we said anything to each other. It was a moment of complete disbelief. Slowly at first, and then like a tsunami, the outrage washed over me.

I opened the door to the living room. My dad sat looking straight ahead. I didn't enter the room. I was calm and measured, but I shook with rage. I had been silent for long enough. I told my dad that I was a good son. That I had got excellent grades at school. I reminded him that I had been the first in our large extended family to go to university. I told him that I worked hard, having had a weekend job since I was sixteen and with my job at the Tron supporting me through university. I pointed out that I never brought problems to the door; I had never been in trouble with the police.

Finally, I appealed to him, 'You have so much to be proud of as my dad. But all you seem to care about is your reputation as a hard man in the shipyards. I've held onto this secret my whole life, and not once have you or mum ever considered the damage and pain this has caused me. Your focus has been on how my sexuality affects you. I don't want to live like this anymore. I need to be free to live my own life. I will not accept you, or anyone, dictating to me how I should live my life. If that means I can no longer live under your roof, then so be it.' Not once did he look at me, instead staring into the middle distance. I closed the door and went upstairs to make a plan.

I made two phone calls: one to a colleague at the Tron who had a room to rent, and another to my friend who lived nearby and owned a car, to ask if he would come and get me. Within an hour, my friend arrived to collect me. While this unfolded, my dad seemed glued to his armchair as I moved like a tornado through the house, removing every trace that I had ever lived there. He did not try to stop me or say anything as I prepared to leave home.

As my friend put the car into gear, with my belongings squashed into every available space, my new, independent life began.

The power of the Mask

I'm sharing this part of my story to explain why my Mask held such a powerful grip over me for most of my life. In Part Three, you'll notice that each of the five leaders I interviewed for this book had a trigger or moment in their early development when they first recall the emergence of the Mask. The realisation in my formative years that I was gay is when, upon reflection, I first observed my Mask as it forced me to keep my sexuality a secret. After I came out to my cousin, I feel I regained some control, no longer fearful of the thoughts the Mask offered me. After all, the first person I'd told about my being gay was incredibly accepting. My colleagues at the Tron accepted my sexuality too, as did my friends at university. The Mask had it all wrong, or so I thought.

When I was outed so hatefully to my parents and I observed their horror and disappointment at my sexuality, the Mask re-emerged. All the thoughts the Mask had offered me as a child came back with gusto.

I left home because I felt my dad was ashamed of me, of my sexuality. When I did this, something changed. My Mask had maintained its control over me with thoughts that made me fearful of rejection by my parents. This rejection was now reality. That negative thought my Mask had offered me as a child had come true. The events surrounding the revelation of my sexuality and me leaving home felt very much like rejection. The Mask had been proven right and, for the next twenty-one years, the Mask became my identity.

Summary

Too many of us wrongly believe we are the Mask. We falsely identify with the Mask, with the mind rather than the Knower. We are not our thoughts, but the silent observer. This belief that we are the Mask is a delusion – a case of mistaken identity.

In sharing my story of how and why I left home, I illustrated how events in our lives can enable the Mask to gain power over us, entrenching its hold and power over our identities. Though I had overcome the Mask's fear of rejection by revealing my sexuality to others, I was later rejected by my parents when they learned of my truth – this gave the Mask back its power over me, as the thoughts it offered me had been proven right.

FIVE
Impact Of The Mask

The Mask can have a wide-ranging impact on our life and affect our leadership abilities. It is important we first understand the Mask's impact at a personal level before we uncover what it can do to our leadership journey. Before we are leaders, we are individuals who grow up, get an education, cope with our first love (and heartbreak), and land our first job. The impact our Mask has on us as we develop into young adults and how we cope with it creates an important foundation and a series of learned responses we can unwittingly carry with us into our executive roles and businesses.

As a child, the Mask offered me thoughts about fear of rejection; as an adult, it offered me rage. I became quick-tempered and aggressive with foes and friends alike. Anything that looked remotely like an attack on me, or my sexuality, was met with instant aggression. I was so angry. Angry with my dad for rejecting me, with society for judging me, with religion for demonising me, and with God for creating me this way. I no longer worried about being rejected as the only people I cared about, my parents, had already rejected me – or so it felt. Fear of rejection had turned to utter outrage at the position I'd found myself in. I began drinking too much, which made me even more aggressive and confrontational. I lost some incredibly dear friends during this time. I was in a downward spiral, thanks to the thoughts, feelings, and actions I was unconsciously accepting from the Mask. As the years rolled by, this pattern of thinking and feeling persisted. Ultimately, it caused me to push my first true love away. He was a sensitive soul and struggled under the full glare of the hard and aggressive person I had become.

By my mid-thirties, I felt I had hit rock bottom. Depression and a lack of direction overwhelmed me. I also suffered a complete collapse of confidence in certain social situations. I would be fine one moment, chatting with friends and then, in an instant, it was like I had fallen through a trapdoor and had no way to climb out. I lost count of the number of times I had to leave social situations abruptly, unable even to talk. I felt numb.

I attended counselling, which briefly helped. It was during a counselling session that I recalled my suicide attempt at age seven. It had been such a traumatic experience that I had suppressed the memory; only with the gentle encouragement of the counsellor did I find the courage to relive it.

Despite this, nothing in counselling helped me to rediscover myself, the person I really was. That didn't happen until I turned forty and met Richard and Liz. Only then did I gain the knowledge and understanding I needed to first expose my Mask and then reject it. I have been rejecting it ever since.

Until then, I didn't know about the Mask. I was living under the delusion that all the negative thoughts in my head represented who I was. That it was my identity. The fear of being rejected for being gay first gave the Mask its tight grip on me, but its power grew ten-fold when I left home because I felt I *had* been rejected by my parents, when I felt that those fears had come to fruition. This made the thoughts in my head seem a credible witness to my actual situation. It cemented the Mask's power over me. It walked in my shoes, as me.

This meant that at the time I started my first business, in 2007, my Mask was still in control of my identity. I was ambitious and driven and wanted to try my hand at running my own business. I began with a small consultancy that offered evaluation services to the global not-for-profit sector. I was successful and ran this business for over thirteen years, winning clients like Oxfam, Doctors Without Borders, Care

International, and the London School of Hygiene and Tropical Medicine.

While outwardly successful, I doubted myself a lot. A large component of working as an evaluator is exposure to academics and writing reports in a scientific, academic style. This is where my Mask tortured me. Whenever it came time to document my findings for a client, my Mask would drench me in fear of not being good enough. It would tell me that I wasn't a true academic and had no right drafting evaluation reports. As a result, the report drafting process was painful. I would agonise over every sentence, every paragraph, often putting so much pressure on myself that I came close to missing deadlines. Given how integral report writing was to the role, my Mask made me hate my work and my business. It robbed me of my confidence as a leader.

In Part Three, the five CEOs I interviewed for this book share their stories of how the Mask has impacted on their leadership. From avoidance of public speaking to decision paralysis at senior team meetings, we shall see how the Mask can erode leadership ability.

Everyone's brought their Mask to work

Let's shift focus now to look at the impact the Mask has at the organisational level. As leaders, we can expose and reject our own Masks, but what about the

Masks of others in the workplace? If everyone has a Mask, the probability that it is going to show up daily in businesses around the globe is high.

How do we recognise the Mask at work? The first step is to ensure you, as the leader, remain conscious and aware of any Mask-related thoughts and feelings within you. You will have a hard time recognising the Mask in others if you are under the control of your own Mask. My Unmasking Plan will support you in this.

By being conscious and observant of the traces the Mask leaves behind, you will begin to recognise other people's Masks. Over time, dependent on the number of direct reports you have, you will identify people's triggers and the typical ways their Masks show up in the workplace. Armed with this insight, you can modify your communication style and, if a team member is already under the spell of their Mask when you are trying to engage them, adopt an approach to get alongside them and de-escalate their threat perception.

Remember, everyone's Mask is different and triggered by different perceived threats. There is more commonality, though, among the types of responses the Mask will generate, typically falling into either fight, flight, or freeze reactions. As the Mask takes control, it projects its presence onto our physical being. For those in 'flight' or 'freeze' modes, the effects can be subtle and difficult to observe. These survival modes attempt to make us shrink, to become invisible to danger, allowing us to retreat. On someone's face, this may look like sadness, with their expression falling. They will become quiet, with nothing to say. Their posture might resemble a hedgehog turning in on itself for protection. Then, when the moment is right, they will skulk away, utterly crestfallen, to lick their wounds and recover from the stress of the perceived attack.

Fight mode, including overt anger and aggression, also shows up on our face and in our physicality. We may narrow our eyebrows in a frown, puff up our chest, our mouth may curl into a scowl. Our voice will increase in volume, perhaps to a shout. Our posture may change as we grow in stature, ready for a fight, moving aggressively towards our target. Unfortunately, this all too often results in physical violence and harm. Even in a professional workplace environment, bullying and intimidation can be common due to Mask-thinking and behaviour. Look out for these indicators in your workplace and recognise them for what they are – a survival response triggered by Mask-thinking.

Of course, when someone's Mask is in control, we must remember that this is most often because it perceives a threat or danger. We will only make matters worse if we continue with whatever approach led to the emergence of their Mask.

While the stories of our five leaders will be shared in full in the next part of the book, to bring Part Two to a close, let's explore some examples they shared of how the Mask can show up in the workplace.

For John, our not-for-profit CEO who we'll meet in Chapter Eight, he recognises the Mask in others particularly when he is met with defensiveness or inflexibility. In managing a situation with a direct report, John recognised that he was dealing with a Mask dictating a 'freeze' survival response. This colleague, let's call her Janet, was being asked to expand her range of outputs, given the organisation's significant growth. Janet likely felt threatened by this and worried that she didn't have the confidence or skills to meet the new challenges of the role. She reacted by ignoring John's requests and continuing to do the job she knew, perhaps hoping that John would forget and the problem would go away.

John also has some experience of the Mask's 'fight' response. Recalling his dealings with an office manager called Mark, he described him as 'defending to the death his way of doing things.' Despite being a lovely person, Mark often upset colleagues. He was so threatened by suggestions that his methods could be improved upon that, as John recalled, he would transform into an almost unrecognisable person who, in acting out their Mask-behaviours, damaged their professional relationships.

Another 'fight' Mask example from John's leadership journey came from the person from whom he took over as CEO. John met his predecessor but didn't have first-hand experience of their worst behaviours. What became clear, as John settled into his new role, was that the former leader needed to belittle and blame people. For John, this meant he had to invest significantly in rebuilding the organisational culture from the ground up. He recalled how morale was 'on the floor' when he took over, with team members unwilling to go beyond their specific roles and responsibilities. His predecessor's Mask had eroded the sense of psychological safety required for strong accountability and for the team to flourish.

John is rightly proud of how he was able to turn the culture around, but recognises that occasionally the fear factor created by the former CEO re-appears in some team members. Despite having left the organisation years ago, the ripple effects of the former leader's Mask are still being felt.

Laura, the accountancy firm Managing Partner who we'll meet in Chapter Nine, sees the Mask in her workplace frequently. In younger partners, whom she considers intelligent and high-flying, she has observed how they can crumble when minor things go wrong. For example, if they receive criticism from a client, when a process goes wrong, or when someone in their team resigns. Laura describes seeing some junior partners 'falling apart' over seemingly nothing.

In Laura's view, she sees a category of ambitious young stars who can fall from sky high to rock bottom when confronted with minor issues. Being a supportive leader, Laura invests considerable time in providing help and reassurance to these colleagues. From this experience, she has learned to be more empathetic in her approach, which is paying dividends. She explains that she has observed Mask-thinking such as: *I'm not a good accountant... I have been promoted too quickly... I'm not an aspiring Managing Partner... I'm not a good leader... I'm in the wrong job... I'm not good enough... I should resign.*

In another example of the Mask in the workplace, Laura shared her experience of managing a partner who, over many years, exhausted all her attempts to support them. When they finally left the business, Laura remembers it as one of the best moments of her professional career.

This partner exhibited bullying and intimidating behaviour with their direct reports and other partners. It was as though their team was working under a cloud, frequently being told what they could not do and were not capable of. It took many months for the affected team to rediscover their worth and potential for growth after the partner left. Rebuilding an environment of psychological safety took time and energy.

After hearing the many examples of Mask-related thinking and behaviour Laura observed in her firm, I asked her how much time in a typical week she spends managing people, versus managing people's Masks. She replied: 'Probably most of my time is spent managing Masks.'

The Mask and team dysfunction

Patrick Lencioni, in his acclaimed book *The 5 Dysfunctions of a Team*, outlines a series of failures in senior leadership teams.[12] The five dysfunctions, according to Lencioni, are:

1. Absence of trust

2. Fear of conflict

3. Lack of commitment

4. Avoidance of accountability

5. Inattention to results

This is an excellent organising framework through which to explore the Mask's impact, which can be seen in each dysfunction. Let's explore the first two: absence of trust and fear of conflict.

Lack of trust can occur when senior team members are reluctant to be vulnerable with each other and so avoid admitting mistakes, exposing weaknesses, or asking for help. Each of these things help to build trust, but from a Mask perspective they are all rooted in fear. In

---

12   PM Lencioni, *The 5 Dysfunctions of a Team* (Random House, 2002)

any senior team, you can guarantee there will be Masks who are fearful of failure, of being found out, of not being good enough. If you have people in your senior team owning the wrong identity (by which I mean a Mask identity), it is likely that there will be a lack of trust in their teams and, hence, they will be dysfunctional.

The second dysfunction, a fear of conflict, is present when senior team members wish to avoid passionate debate. The clue is in the word 'fear', which puts us squarely in Mask territory. If senior teams comprise people who are owning their Mask identities, the probability is that some will fear conflict and seek to avoid it at all costs. Let me be clear, Lencioni doesn't mean Mask-based conflict, involving aggression and anger, but ideological conflict to ensure that strategic decisions have been thoroughly tested before implementation. He is referring to consciously entering conflict discourse. Left unchecked, Masks avoiding ideological conflict can result in poor decision making, which benefits no one.

The remaining dysfunctions – lack of commitment, avoidance of accountability and inattention to detail – all flow from the first two dysfunctions. If you recognise any of the dysfunctions described here in your senior team, the likelihood is that they are owning their Mask identities. This might not be all the time, it could be infrequent even, but at your next leadership meeting be on the lookout for Mask-thinking, feelings, and actions. I guarantee that you'll find them.

Summary

As the Mask is always in a place of fear, the thoughts, feelings, and actions it offers you are highly likely to have a negative impact on your leadership and life. In my case, the Mask has cost me friendships and robbed me of a deserved sense of achievement.

Each of the five CEOs who contributed to this book recognise that the Mask has held them back in the past and may still be holding them back in different ways now. From decision-making paralysis to avoidance of specific leadership tasks, each of our leaders has suffered from owning the wrong identity.

At the organisational level, we must recognise that everyone brings their Mask to work. At the senior leadership level, we can use Patrick Lencioni's five dysfunctions as an organising framework to identify and understand how the Mask undermines decision making, affecting culture and productivity.

PART THREE
BEAT THE MASK

In this last part of the book, my aim is to set out a simple plan to help you unmask your true identity – the confident leader within. The plan has a series of steps to take to beat your Mask and minimise the impact of other people's Masks on your business and life.

In Chapter Six I'll outline the key steps to the Unmasking Plan. Then, in the last five chapters, I will present a series of case studies from five highly successful leaders. I will focus on the emergence of their Mask, including understanding when and how the Mask first showed up in their lives and endeavour to identify what contextual factors may have influenced their Masks in early life. I will explore the impact the Mask has had on their leadership and lives and apply my three-step plan for beating the Mask to each leader's case.

SIX

The Unmasking Plan

There are three main steps to unmasking your true identity. The Unmasking Plan is illustrated in Figure 3. You'll note that the three steps of the plan rest upon four cornerstones. Let me begin with these.

In Chapter One, I asked you a favour. I asked you to trust in the process and to accept the ideas I present in this book as 'truths'. These truths are the four cornerstones of the Unmasking Plan:

1. We all have a Mask.

2. The Mask is a fictional character of the mind, representing any thoughts, feelings, or actions that we wouldn't consciously choose.

3. We are not the Mask.

4. We cannot get rid of the Mask.

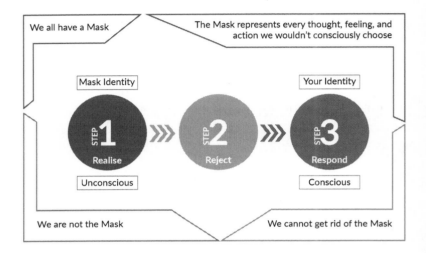

The Unmasking Plan

The first cornerstone truth is that we all have a Mask. Every person on the planet has one. They might not call it the Mask, preferring terms such as 'negative voice', 'the ego', or 'saboteur'. They may not call it anything. They might not know it is there at all. In any case, they have one.

The second cornerstone is acceptance of what the Mask symbolises. Remember, the Mask is driven by psychological fear – nothing it offers you will serve you in a positive way. The third cornerstone is acceptance that you are not the Mask. While the Mask has the power to assume our identity, it is not who we are.

When the Mask is in control, we have a case of mistaken identity. We have become unconscious and left an opening for the Mask to take over. When we fail to consciously choose how we want to think, feel, and act, the Mask can assume our identity.

The final cornerstone is acceptance that we cannot get rid of the Mask. No matter how hard we try, it will always be there, lurking in our subconscious. Knowing that our Mask is ever present makes it even more important to implement the Unmasking Plan. Although we cannot get rid of our Mask, we can become experts at realising when it is in control, at rejecting what it offers us, and at responding consciously to maintain our identity.

While we all have a Mask, the extent to which it impacts our lives varies. There are many factors influencing this, but I'm going to focus on just two main themes. The first is a complex set of factors that I will bundle together and describe as 'the context of your formative years'. By this I mean where you were born, your gender, sexuality, socioeconomic status, educational opportunities, health, your parents/guardians, and any significant events, including trauma. These factors are vast and unique to you, as illustrated in my story and those of the five leaders I interviewed for this book.

The second factor is the false belief that we are the Mask. When we wrongly identify with the Mask, we unwittingly hand control over to this fictional character of the mind that knows only fear.

Let's now explore the plan's three steps, which are:

1. **Realise** when your Mask is in control
2. **Reject** the thoughts, feelings and actions the Mask offers
3. **Respond** consciously

The following sections will discuss each of these in more detail.

Step 1: Realise

For most of our day, we are on autopilot. We wake up, take a shower, get dressed, and prepare breakfast, with little conscious thought. We find our way to work, whether driving or on public transport, with minimal effort.

We only become conscious if something disrupts our routine, for example if we are travelling to an unfamiliar location, or we have to take a different route because of closed roads, traffic, or public transport issues. When we arrive at work, we go through the routine of greeting our colleagues and fall into the pattern of doing our job. Depending on the complexity of our work, we might need to become conscious to solve complex problems, or for creativity. For more repetitive work, though, our learned patterns and routines take over. At the end of the day, we do everything in reverse – we travel home, prepare a meal, brush our teeth, and go to bed.

Neuroscientists estimate we are only conscious of what we're doing for approximately 5% of the average day.[13] This means we are unconscious and unaware of what we are thinking, feeling, and doing most days. This gives the Mask vast opportunity in your average day to assume your identity.

Realising your Mask is in control requires you to have greater awareness of your thoughts, feelings, and actions. This takes practice but gets easier the more you do it. The first sign that our Mask is in control might be a feeling. For example, you could become aware that you're feeling anxious, angry, sad, guilty, or jealous. The table below lists some common Mask-generated feelings.

Hatred	Anxiety	Hurt	Fear
Worry	Contempt	Envy	Anger
Rage	Despair	Hopelessness	Nervousness
Hostility	Jealousy	Annoyance	Disgust
Shame	Guilt	Loneliness	Aggression
Anguish	Aversion	Bitterness	Resentment
Dejection	Depression	Disappointment	Dislike
Dismay	Embarrassment	Misery	Grumpiness
Weakness	Humiliation	Indignance	Insecurity
Infuriation	Loathing	Irritation	Outrage

(Continued)

13   J Kluger, 'You're pretty much unconscious all of the time', *Time Magazine* (26 June 2015), https://time.com/3937351/consciousness-unconsciousness-brain, accessed April 2023

(cont.)

Hatred	Anxiety	Hurt	Fear
Pity	Pessimism	Powerlessness	Rejection
Remorse	Fear	Self-pity	Smugness
Spite	Sullenness	Tension	Vengefulness

Whatever the feeling may be, the important question to ask of yourself is: *Would I choose to feel this way?* As the Mask only ever offers feelings that are based on fear, a bad feeling is a sure sign that the Mask is in control.

It might take you a bit of practice to become conscious of how you are feeling. You may have spent an entire day feeling bad and only notice many hours or days later. It doesn't matter how long it takes to realise that negative feelings are present; what matters is that you eventually become aware of how you are feeling.

The instant you become aware of a bad feeling, you become conscious and present. Let me emphasise this point: if you are feeling bad, then you are unconscious. We know this because you *wouldn't consciously choose to feel bad*. When you are feeling bad, the Mask is in control and assuming your identity. The moment you observe a negative feeling, you move from *being* the feeling (where your Mask is in control), to *observing* the feeling (where you are in control). In doing so, you dissociate from the Mask.

As you observe the emotion offered to you by the Mask, you may find its intensity diminish. Whether internally, or aloud, you can then ask questions like: *I wouldn't choose to feel anxious – what has led to me feeling this way? Feeling this way does not serve me positively – what has brought me here?* This will help you to consider the thoughts that gave rise to the feeling. Feelings are the body's response to thoughts. Anxious feelings begin as anxious thoughts.

In a deeply unconscious state, we may only realise the Mask is in charge at the level of action. Perhaps we react angrily to a colleague who has disturbed our concentration by approaching our desk uninvited. Or we shrink back from contributing to a meeting, for fear of saying something 'stupid'. We wouldn't consciously choose to respond in these ways – a clear sign the Mask is in the driving seat.

Other tell-tale symptoms of the Mask being in control include comparing yourself with others. In Chapter Eleven, you will meet Mark, a college principal. Mark's Mask often compares him with other people, leaving him feeling inadequate. Comparing yourself to others often leads to feelings of insufficiency. Typical Mask-thinking readily acknowledges other people's strengths, but compares them with your weaknesses – hardly a fair analysis.

Acting like a petulant child, throwing a tantrum and slamming doors is also Mask territory. This might sound absurd, but I have seen plenty of adults behaving like this when they don't get their way, for example when they lose an argument or feel attacked when colleagues challenge their ideas. The initial outburst is often followed by withdrawal and a refusal to engage.

Realising that your Mask is in control is the first step to beating it. This takes practice, but trust me, you will get faster at recognising your Mask and spend less time in its clutches. As you begin to practise recognising when your Mask is in control, use Castillo's model to expose your Mask's identity by identifying the thoughts, feelings, and actions that are unique to your Mask. Try the following exercise to see how this looks in practice.

EXERCISE: Expose the Mask

On a piece of paper, or digitally, create a list like the one shown below. You can begin at any of the stages and work forwards or backwards to reveal your Mask's identity. For example, you might begin with a result that you recently experienced that you believe is because of your Mask. Let's use an example from John, our non-profit leader who you'll meet in Chapter Eight. John's Mask fears failure. This used to lead him to avoid speaking or presenting in public, which meant he would encourage colleagues to present his work instead of him, and they would get the praise and recognition.

- **Circumstances:** John's leadership roles often required him to present and speak in public.
- **Thoughts:** John had thoughts such as... *I don't know enough... I'll be found out... I have nothing important to say.*
- **Feelings:** John experienced anxiety and panic attacks.

- **Actions:** John opted out, leaving colleagues to make presentations.
- **Results:** John's colleagues received the praise for his work.

Using John's example, if we begin at the level of the result – his colleagues getting praise for his work – and work backwards to the action that led to this result, we see that John opted out of speaking in public, avoiding it at all costs and giving the opportunity to his colleagues. Mapping back to the feelings that precede that action, we can see that he often experienced anxiety related to public speaking, sometimes accompanied by panic attacks. Going back further, we get to the thoughts that caused that anxiety, including imposter thoughts such as *I'll be found out*.

The above exercise is a useful method you can use to expose your Mask's identity, using authentic examples from your leadership and life. When you have an awareness of the various circumstances that trigger your Mask, and the typical thoughts and feelings your Mask generates, it will be easier to more quickly recognise when your Mask is in control.

EXERCISE: Monitoring your internal state

When you put this first step of the plan into action, it's helpful to find a way of regularly monitoring your internal state. An easy way of doing this is to set an alarm on your phone that goes off several times a day with a prompt that reminds you to become conscious and present. For variety, you can choose different prompts for different times of day. Here are some examples:

- Remember to choose today!
- What's going on inside right now?
- You are not the Mask; you are the Knower.
- Is your current thinking serving you positively?
- How are you feeling right now? Would you choose to feel this way?
- Are you choosing right now?
- The Mask only knows fear. What are you thinking and feeling right now?

Don't fall into the trap of thinking that allowing your Mask to be in control is a failure – it is not. That is Mask-thinking. The Mask is a powerful part of our subconscious survival response that has evolved with us over hundreds of thousands of years. Learning to recognise when the Mask is in control will take time and practice. What's important is that you keep trying – and remember, as soon you realise you are experiencing Mask thoughts, feelings, and actions, you are no longer under its spell and have become conscious and present. You can now move to the second step of the Unmasking Plan: Reject.

Step 2: Reject

Realising the Mask is in control has brought you back into consciousness. Now it's time to reject whatever thoughts, feelings, and actions the Mask is offering you – these are rooted in psychological fear. The basis is *always* fear. Fear of rejection. Fear of failure. Fear of loss. Fear of pain. The list of possible fears is endless. The fears the Mask projects onto us are either related to the past or the future. If they come from the past, this can lead to feelings of sadness, resentment, and depression; if they're related to the future, worry and anxiety are common. The Mask doesn't live in the present – it is a time traveller. Knowing this is a crucial weapon in defeating it.

Your Mask may keep taking you back to the past to relive historic trauma or remind you of your regrets. Regret is an interesting Mask feeling. The regret itself is offered to you by the Mask in the now, despite the event or decision it relates to occurring in the past, for you to relive in all its excruciating detail. Moreover, it is highly likely that it was Mask-thinking that caused the historic regret. This makes regret a double-whammy for the Mask.

In *The Power of Regret*, Daniel Pink usefully categorises regrets into four themes.[14] Foundation regrets encompass regrets related to actions needed to move forward but avoided. Boldness regrets relate to opportunities not taken. Moral regrets are about not doing the 'right' thing, while connection regrets concern people lost from our lives, for whatever reason.

For foundation regrets, the Mask may offer thoughts like: *I should have done the work? Why didn't I complete*

---

14   DH Pink, *The Power of Regret* (Canongate Books, 2022)

the report on time? For boldness regrets: *If only I'd taken the chance. Why didn't I leap at the opportunity?* For moral regrets: *I should have done the right thing. I am a bad person.* For connection regrets: *Why did I not reach out sooner? They were a good friend to me.*

In each of the above examples, the Mask had likely been at work planting the seed for the future regret. In the foundation regret example, you failed to do a piece of work on time. But what caused you to slip up and miss the deadline? In the boldness regret example, not taking chances and risks is often because of Mask-based fear. The moral regret is almost certainly caused by the Mask, as no conscious person would choose to do the wrong thing. Finally, in the connection regret example, might Mask-thinking be a contributing factor in why this person is no longer in your life?

The Mask may wield this power over you because of internal resistance, a reluctance to accept events or situations in your life. Feeling regret, sadness and resentment could be a sign that your Mask is taking you back to the past.

The Mask also transports us to the future where it paints vivid pictures of problems and scenarios that might never happen. Even if such issues could arise in the future, they are not happening right now, so why worry about them? Would you choose to worry about something that might never happen?

While the Mask is in control, taking us backwards and forwards in time, we cannot be conscious in the present. The Mask robs us of our identity, heaps misery upon us, and, through its fear-induced time travel, robs us of the one real thing we have – this moment, here, right now.

The table of thoughts

Spiritual leaders tell us to simply observe our thoughts and feelings, not analyse or judge them. In practice, I have found this challenging, particularly at the start of my journey to beat the Mask. Recognising this, I want to provide some techniques for not over-analysing Mask-related thoughts and feelings that can support you to have an internal dialogue with the Mask, to help quell its power over you.

As we have seen in Castillo's model, feelings and actions start out as thoughts. Our thinking is at the root of everything. If our starting point is a negative thought, offered by the Mask, the likelihood of a positive result is low. When it comes to thoughts, the Mask has an advantage over us: speed. As the Mask is hardwired into our survival system, operating at the subconscious level, its reaction time is several seconds faster than our conscious self.[15]

---

15 'Conscious vs subconscious processing power', *Spd Rdng* (26 August 2009), https://spdrdng.com/posts/conscious-vs-subconscious-processing, accessed April 2023

To counteract this, envision all the thoughts you could ever possibly think laid out on a vast table in your mind. This immense table contains thoughts we may consider positive, negative, and neutral. You can consciously choose whatever thoughts you want from this table. Everything on it is always available to you – that is, to the Knower within you. You as pure consciousness, devoid of the Mask and separate from the mind.

As we approach the table of thoughts to make our selection, the shadowy figure of the Mask stands before us, blocking our way. The Mask arrived at the table before us and selected thoughts for us – all negative, all drenched in fear, and all unlikely to serve us in any positive way. As we try to get to the table of thoughts ourselves, the Mask forces us to consider the thoughts it is offering. We acquiesce and, depending on what those thoughts are, we may already be feeling a wave of negative emotions. For example, if we see the thought *I'm not good enough*, we may already be feeling defeated. Sometimes, we may turn the thoughts into actions and only recognise the bad feeling afterwards. Consider how the thought *he's ridiculing me in front of my colleagues* could quickly lead to an argument, where you only feel the anger as the conflict escalates.

Back at the table of thoughts, we haven't yet moved past the Mask to make our own selection. The Mask may have pushed thoughts on us that trigger feelings and then actions (that we would not have consciously chosen) before we've even reached the table. If we do not reject the thoughts offered to us by the Mask, then we accept them by default. The Mask stays in control, assuming our identity. We never reach the table of thoughts, and we remain unconscious. In this scenario, the only way to choose consciously is to reject what the Mask is offering and step up to the table.

Discredit the witness

If the Mask were a living person, we wouldn't trust it or believe a single word it uttered. This is how we must treat the Mask. We must reject it as an unreliable witness. A liar.

Let's quickly recap. You find yourself in a situation that has triggered your Mask. By practising Step One of the Unmasking Plan, you realise your Mask is in control because you are thinking, feeling, or acting in a way that you wouldn't choose to. This realisation has brought you into consciousness.

How do you now reject the thoughts being offered to you by the Mask? Let's be mindful that in realising your Mask was in control, you are, to an extent, already feeling its ill effects, whether that's negative thinking, feeling bad, or acting in ways you wouldn't choose. This can make it challenging to snap back control from the Mask. For example, if you are feeling angry in the throes of an argument, the momentum can make it seem easier to continue with this behaviour. But that would leave the Mask in charge.

After implementing Step One, you will already be more present. You must now continue to be the Knower, observing the Mask-thinking. The simplest way to reject the Mask is to turn your attention away from whatever it is offering you. Where we place our attention is where our energy flows. Hence, acknowledging but then turning attention away from the thoughts, feelings, and actions the Mask wants you to engage in and towards your breathing, for example, will turn down the volume of that voice.

When we find it difficult to draw attention away from the Mask, it can be helpful to have a conversation with it, either internally or, if you are in a private space, aloud as though the Mask were in the room with you. Before we explore some useful conversational strategies, note that a positive result is more likely if you are prepared to consciously accept certain situations in your life, without resistance. For example, you have missed a train and will now be late for an important meeting; you treated a colleague poorly and unprofessionally, resulting in them leaving the firm; your sales targets are off track and you may need to lay people off; your divorce has left you with mountains of debt and you have to start anew. These examples could be facts in anyone's life. Several of them have been situations I've faced. These facts are neither good nor bad, they just 'are'. They only become good or bad for us depending on how we process them.

All the above examples are likely to trigger the Mask, setting off a stream of thoughts and feelings that will only harm you. Be careful. When you are in a hole, you don't get out of it by continuing to dig. If you consciously accept the situation, however awful it may first appear, you will take the Mask's power away.

So you've missed your sales targets. That is unfortunate, but it's better that you accept it than worry about it. Worrying doesn't change the sales figures and is harming you. You've missed your only train and you have no other options that allow you to make the meeting on time. Why beat yourself up? It won't help you get to the meeting, but it will make you feel awful. The divorce may have left you in debt, but getting mad about it, blaming others, or regretting ever getting married in the first place changes nothing. You are still in debt.

Why put the Mask in the driving seat? I can guarantee it will make you feel worse, while changing nothing about your situation. Better you remain calm and in control. You'll be more likely to find a way through the challenge and feel better about doing it, too.

With the intention to accept whatever situation you may face, you can have a conversation with the Mask. Often, telling the Mask you have heard it is enough to quieten its voice. The conversation may go something like this:

MASK: The head of operations doesn't like me. Who does he think he is? I am his superior; he should show me respect. I should put him in his place, remind him who's boss.

YOU: I hear your concerns, but I do not share them. Whether he likes me is none of my concern. My priority is to remain professional.

MASK: But I will appear weak if I don't bring him down. Show him who's boss, or he will come after my job.

YOU: I hear your concerns, but I do not share them. I am confident about my position and my abilities. I need you to be quiet now. You offer me nothing that I want.

After your conversation with the Mask, move your attention away from its voice. Acknowledge it, counter its argument, but move on.

My Mask can be extreme. Often, its advice for solving the most mundane of problems is for me to kill myself. Let's say a meeting hasn't gone as well as expected. My Mask will try to erode my confidence, starting with the 'bad' meeting, then reminding me of all the bad things in the world, how humanity is full of hate. My Mask is determined to kill me. Faced with such extreme negative thoughts, I have found it effective to ridicule the Mask. Here is a typical conversation I might have with it:

MASK: That meeting didn't go well. They think I'm incompetent. My business isn't going to get any better; in fact, it's never going to get better. The economy is so bleak right now. The war in Ukraine is so awful. The world really is a terrible place...

ME: Ha! I suppose I should kill myself? That's your answer to everything.

MASK: [Silence]

ME: I will choose to keep everything in perspective. One bad meeting is not the end of the world.

To discredit the Mask, treat it like a witness in a courtroom. Put it on the stand and try cross-examining it.

MASK: I'm going to get found out. I don't know what I'm doing. I'm a failure.

YOU: How can I be a failure? I am highly qualified with a twenty-year career in successively senior roles. I lead an award-winning organisation that has doubled its turnover in my short tenure. I am successful.

MASK: But what if that all changes? It could come crashing down tomorrow.

YOU: Worrying about 'what-ifs' does not serve me positively. I have been successful – and I will continue to be successful.

To beat the Mask, CEO John starts by acknowledging it, which helps to silence it. He may have a conversation with the Mask to help lessen its intensity. He also finds positive self-talk helpful, recognising that he is successful, that he has something positive to say and contribute. Self-care is part of his approach to rejecting the Mask, including taking time out from work, whether full holidays or brief breaks.

Step 3: Respond

By following the first two steps you will realise when the Mask is in control and be able to reject what it offers you. This supports you to become conscious, wrestle back control from the Mask, and regain your identity. Now it's time to choose.

This might sound outrageously simple, but if you want to be a confident leader, then you are a confident leader. Choose confident thoughts and confident feelings and confident actions will flow. Move away from what the Mask is offering you and choose what you want. When the Mask is in control, we react. When we are in control, we respond. Reaction involves no thought, no consciousness, just fear.[16] Responding involves you becoming present, rejecting the Mask's suggestions, and consciously choosing what you want to think, how you want to feel and act. The last step of the Unmasking Plan is about moving from reacting to responding.

In any situation, you have two choices. Either you remain unconscious and let the Mask react out of fear, offering you thoughts, feelings, and actions that will not serve you, or you reject the Mask and make a conscious, positive choice. When you operate at this level of consciousness, it appears absurd to facilitate Mask-thinking. If we have the choice between believing we are a failure or a success, I know what choice I'd make – success, every time.

The table below contains a list of Mask-thoughts in the left-hand column, and conscious responses to these

---

16 J Taylor, 'The difference between reacting and responding', *Psychology Today* (5 October 2021), www.psychologytoday.com/gb/blog/the-power-prime/202110/the-difference-between-reacting-and-responding, accessed April 2023

in the righthand column. You might recognise some of the thoughts your Mask offers you. Which list do you – the Knower within you – want to choose from?

The Mask (reacting)	You (responding)
I can't do this	I can do this
I don't have enough experience	I have enough experience
I'm not a confident person	I am a confident person
I'm afraid of public speaking	I enjoy public speaking
I have nothing to say	I have as much to say as anyone else
I am not enough	I am enough
I am a failure	I am successful
I don't deserve love	I deserve love
I am not strong	I am strong
I am not intelligent	I am intelligent
I am ugly	I am beautiful
I am lazy	I am motivated
I am disliked	I am liked
I am undeserving	I am deserving
I am stressed	I am relaxed
I am impatient	I am patient
I am a victim	I am the victor
I am angry	I am at peace
I am useless	I am useful
I am a fraud	I am authentic

I find Stoic philosophy particularly useful in responding consciously to situations. Stoicism has its foundations in the third century BCE, with Epictetus being one of its most well-known proponents. Born a Roman slave, he later became one of the great Stoic teachers and philosophers. In his essay 'The Enchiridion', he reminds us of an important tenet of Stoic philosophy – that of distinguishing between what we can and cannot control.[17]

In essence, we only have control over our inner world – this is our thoughts, feelings, and actions. Anything external, including the actions of others, is beyond our control. This means that no one has the power to ruin your day or make you feel bad. It's always an inside job. Only you can control your inner world, through how you choose to respond. RuPaul Charles, of Drag Race fame, made this point neatly when he said, 'What other people think of me is none of my business.'[18]

If the only control we have is that over our inner world, it is a human tragedy if we allow the Mask to assume our identity and take this control away. For if we do not have control of our thoughts, feelings, and actions, then we are lost.

---

17 'Who is Epictetus? From slave to world's most sought after philosopher', *Daily Stoic* (no date), https://dailystoic.com/epictetus, accessed April 2023

18 R Charles (@RuPaul) 'What other people think...' (2 March 2011), https://twitter.com/RuPaul/status/42738850195439617, accessed April 2023

Accessing the treasure chest

Answer this question honestly: what do you hold onto the longest, a compliment or a criticism? I suspect most people reading this book will say the latter. Many of us need practice accessing the various positive thoughts and feelings we have within us. Know this: every feeling that you can possibly experience is already inside you. No external event or person delivers joy to you; this joy is always inside you. All that happens externally is that you perceive something or someone as giving you permission to access the feeling of joy that you already possess. But you have access to it all the time, whenever you choose.

If every feeling is already inside us, through responding consciously we can learn how to access this emotional treasure chest. Too many people postpone future happiness, saying things like, 'I will feel confident as a leader when we double our turnover.' I can promise you this: no one hands you the feeling of confidence. It lies within you at all times.

Why deny yourself the feeling of confidence today? If you think and feel confident right now, your likelihood of success in the future is greater than if you postpone the feeling of confidence until you 'get there'. You are already there.

Identifying ways to access your treasure chest can help you increase your consciousness and ensure you move from reacting (the Mask) to responding (you). The exercise below will help you to access the feeling of joy.

EXERCISE: Accessing your treasure chest

Grab a notepad and list all the things you can do that give you joy. All the things that feed your soul, that bring a smile to your face. With your list complete, implement a plan to weave as many of your treasure chest activities into your days and weeks as you can. Here are some examples to inspire you:

- Going for a walk in nature
- Working out at the gym
- Listening to uplifting music
- Watching comedies
- Going for a run or a cycle
- Attending live music performances
- Hanging out with friends
- Singing in a local amateur choir
- Learning new skills, eg cooking
- Volunteering for a good cause
- Meditating

Summary

This chapter introduced the three-step Unmasking Plan to beat your Mask, which rests upon four cornerstone truths. Step One is to realise when the Mask has assumed our identity; often, this is indicated by feeling bad, comparing ourselves with others, or acting like a child. As soon as we notice how we are feeling, we have become conscious, and the Mask is no longer in control.

Step Two is to reject the thoughts, feelings, and actions offered by the Mask. We have learned that the Mask has a speed advantage over our conscious selves and so can select from the 'table of thoughts' before we have time to engage. To fully reject the Mask, we must first acknowledge and observe what it is offering. One way to do this is to have a conversation with the Mask and, through this, discredit what it is saying. The final step in the Unmasking Plan is to move from reacting to responding to situations in a conscious way to prevent the Mask from assuming our identity and to remain in control.

We took some lessons from Stoic philosophy to serve as useful reminders that we only have control over our internal world and that no person or situation has the power to ruin our day unless we allow it.

Finally, we learned about the treasure chest inside us containing every possible human feeling we can or will ever experience, which we can access whenever we want. Most of us are experts at accessing negative feelings, thanks to the power of the Mask, but by identifying things we can do to access our positive feelings instead, we can learn to give ourselves permission to feel confident and successful right now.

SEVEN
The Not-For-Profit Leader

It is now time to meet our five leaders and discover how their Masks first emerged and the impact they had on their leadership journeys. Given the sensitive nature of the subject, I have anonymised each contributor, changing names, genders, and sectors.

I have structured each case study to mirror how I have presented the learnings in the book. In each of the five case studies, we begin by exposing the Mask; we then explore the impact of the Mask on their leadership and life, and end by applying the Unmasking Plan. We begin with John.

Exposing the Mask: John's story

John is the CEO of a UK national charity with over 200 staff. His career to date has been exclusively in service of the not-for-profit sector and he has held various leadership roles over the past twenty years. I consider John to be a highly competent, confident, and inspiring leader.

John first noticed his Mask somewhere around the age of ten, while at primary school. He recalls being in the playground and acting in ways that left him not feeling good about himself. I asked John if he could remember what his Mask sounded like back then, what it would say to him. After a brief hesitation, he explained that his Mask would say things like: *I'm rubbish... No one wants to play with me... No one likes me*, and... *I'm so stupid*. John's Mask sounds as harsh as mine did at this age.

Reflecting on how the Mask used to speak to him back then, John recognises that the comments were quiet childish judgements about 'stupid things', but that they built up in his head and became quite destructive, both at the time and for many years afterwards. He remembers how the Mask-thoughts affected his behaviour at school, where he started putting up defences. The thoughts John's Mask offered him back then led to him having feelings of, in his own words, 'complete worthlessness'. He didn't feel anywhere near good enough and had the sense that he was failing in everything, all the time.

These feelings and the sense of failure at school set off a fresh wave of Mask-related thoughts, such as *screw you and everybody else too*. This in turn triggered feelings of anger and defensiveness, which resulted in John finding a new way of coping with the world. He determined at a young age that he would not rely on anyone, not ask for help, and not show any weakness. He would withdraw from those around him and go his own way. Because of his Mask-thinking, he did the bare minimum at school and left with virtually no qualifications.

You'll recall that in exposing the Mask, it is important to understand its identity, revealed through the thoughts, feelings, and actions it typically offers. As these are typically rooted in fear, it is useful to determine what specifically the Mask is fearful of. In John's case, his Mask appeared fearful of rejection. This Mask-thinking led to him checking out of school, of friendship, activities, and aspects of his home life. John's Mask justified its position using utterly perverse logic: that if he withdrew and didn't engage, he wouldn't expose himself to failure and, ultimately, rejection.

Looking back, John realises that this way of thinking denied him opportunities and growth, with him missing out on life chances and experiences that he would have otherwise enjoyed. His Mask has cost him relationships and friendships that he can never get back. The Mask made John's life more difficult than it had to be; as a result of Mask-thinking, he didn't let people in, rejecting them before they rejected him. John believes all this stemmed from the thought, put in his head by the Mask, that he was not good enough and never would be. He realises now that these thoughts were the catalyst for everything that followed. John told me, 'It led to thoughts like, *Why bother trying, I'm only going to let everyone down.'*

The Mask had a destructive influence on John for around ten years after he left primary school. He recalls being 'driven by it' because he was young and didn't understand what the Mask was, or even that he had one. Like so many of us, he lacked the life experience to reflect on it at that young age.

The turning point for John came when he was studying for a counselling qualification after leaving secondary school. The course contained an element of reflective practice and helped him to understand the difference between conscious thoughts and those thoughts offered to him by his Mask. Yet the realisation of the effects the Mask had had on him was still too painful for him to acknowledge properly. John believes it took another ten years before he confronted it. In his own words, 'I knew it was there, but I just didn't want to look at it.'

When we reflect as adults, we often find that the emergence of our Mask is associated with traumatic moments, or painful events in early life. For John, when he was old enough, he came to realise that his upbringing had been atypical.

John's father left the family unit to be with a partner he had been having an affair with, when John was just six years old. But even before his father finally left the family home, he was emotionally absent. John felt like an unwelcome addition, having been born into this situation, and that he'd ultimately been rejected when his father left. In further support of this, John's older brother had a good relationship with their father, while John and his father had failed to bond.

John's mother, perhaps in response to the collapse of her marriage, then changed her lifestyle, deciding to spend more time socialising and leaving the children at home alone. As a result, John felt like he had lost both his parents at a young age; he learned the pain of rejection early in his development. To make matters worse, other children at his school picked up on the unfortunate change in his circumstances and used it to make fun of him.

While this was all unfolding, John's Mask was observing, looking for danger. The pain John felt from the perceived rejection by first his father and then his mother was interpreted by his Mask as life-threatening, putting it on high alert.

For the avoidance of doubt, I'm not saying that rejection can't be painful. It is. Research shows that the same regions of our brain are involved when we feel social exclusion as when we feel physical pain.[19] The avoidance of physical pain is an important survival response, but the brain doesn't distinguish between physical pain and the emotional pain of social rejection. This is because we have evolved to be social mammals. Early in our evolution, it was crucial to be part of the tribe, as this increased our likelihood of survival – we benefitted from the collective protection of the group and had better access to food and resources. In our modern world, though, social rejection is no longer the difference between life and death, even if it might feel like it. Rejection is now something we must learn to cope with to become resilient individuals. We experience rejection throughout our lives, from unreciprocated love to not being chosen by the rugby team. Strength comes from learning to cope with rejection and move forward.

---

19 G MacDonald and MR Leary, 'Why does social exclusion hurt? The relationship between social and physical pain', *Psychological Bulletin*, 131/2 (2005), pp202–223, https://doi.org/10.1037/0033-2909.131.2.202, accessed April 2023

In recounting his story, John can rationalise the emergence of his Mask and everything associated with it, yet he finds acknowledging the part he's played in this much more difficult. This struck a chord with me, as I have had similar struggles. Yes, understanding the Mask can help us explain negative thoughts, feelings, and actions, to see why we might have reacted angrily to a friend who was just in the wrong place at the wrong time. Yet, while the Mask helps to explain negative behaviour, it doesn't excuse it. We must still acknowledge the part we played and make amends for any harm we may have caused. If the Mask is in control, it is because we have allowed it to be. We have facilitated the Mask by not consciously choosing more appropriate behaviour. Whenever we have let the Mask be in control, we must accept responsibility for the outcome.

John's Mask identity

Let's now apply Castillo's coaching model to the emergence of John's Mask.

Circumstances: John's father left the family unit to be with another woman. John and his father had never bonded. After John's father moved out, his mother began socialising more, often leaving him and his brother home alone. Children at John's school teased him about his home life.

Thoughts: In response to John's circumstances, his Mask offered him thoughts like: *I'm not good enough... No one likes me... I'm so stupid... I'm failing at everything, all the time... I'm rubbish... No one wants to play with me.*

Feelings: Feeling rejected by his parents, John's Mask-thinking produced a fear of rejection by his school friends and of being found out as 'not clever enough'. It initially generated feelings of anxiety and complete worthlessness, and later on anger and defensiveness.

Behaviours/actions: Feeling this way led to John checking out at school, doing just the bare minimum to get by. He also withdrew from friendship groups. He stopped asking for help, adopting a 'screw you' attitude that pushed people away.

Results: John left school with virtually no qualifications and experienced social isolation.

Impact of John's Mask

Understanding John's story, including his perception of losing his parents at a young age, partly explains his Mask's identity. John's dad leaving the family home to be with another woman and his mother's decision to lead a more active social life, resulting in him being left home alone, elicited in him a deep sense of rejection.

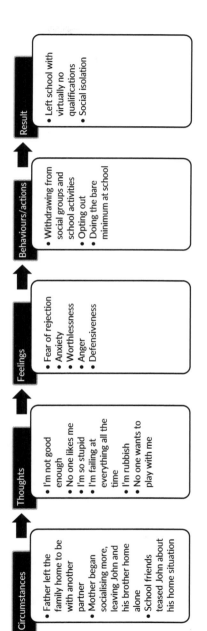

Circumstances	Thoughts	Feelings	Behaviours/actions	Result
• Father left the family home to be with another partner • Mother began socialising more, leaving John and his brother home alone • School friends teased John about his home situation	• I'm not good enough • No one likes me • I'm so stupid • I'm failing at everything all the time • I'm rubbish • No one wants to play with me	• Fear of rejection • Anxiety • Worthlessness • Anger • Defensiveness	• Withdrawing from social groups and school activities • Opting out • Doing the bare minimum at school	• Left school with virtually no qualifications • Social isolation

Exposing John's Mask

John now recognises that, in his leadership role, his Mask gets triggered when he doesn't feel fully in control, or on top of an issue or situation. Maybe he doesn't feel he has all the facts, or he can't control the timings of an event or meeting, or things aren't unfolding as per the plan in his head. John feels that this is when his Mask is at its most destructive. The thoughts the Mask offers John in these situations are along the lines of: *I should know this, why don't I know this? I have failed somewhere along the line because I don't know this back-to-front and upside down... I'm going to get found out... I'm rubbish.*

All these thoughts contribute to John feeling that he is not good enough, that he should be better than he is. John consciously recognises that what his Mask is suggesting is impossible and completely unnecessary. He acknowledges, 'I can't possibly know everything about any subject or issue as it arises.' John accepts that some thoughts his Mask typically offers him, including of not being good enough, are evident in both of his parents. He describes how his mother in particular was 'chronically disabled' by such thoughts for much of her life, whereas the drive to be better, in response to not feeling good enough, comes from his father. To some extent, John accepts that he likely inherited these Mask-thoughts and feelings directly from his parents. John has made peace with this. Though while he no longer feels the painful sting of rejection by his parents, he still remembers what it felt like, and the subconscious programming of his Mask has been fixed, leaving him to deal with the consequences of the choices it has made for him over the years. He can see the ripple effects everywhere. When he gets together with his old school friends and they reminisce about the fun times they used to have, John doesn't remember any of them. Yet he can recall with utter clarity the negative events in his life, along with the stress they caused. These memories are so much more powerful.

Reviewing John's leadership journey, there are clear traces of his Mask throughout. For example, he used to avoid 'like the plague' speaking in public, whether that was at an event or conference or a small room of four or five people, yet the nature of John's career has required him to speak in public often. For weeks prior to a speaking event, John describes experiencing a deep sense of dread, despite being an expert in his subject and well known to the people who would make up the audience. The feeling of dread sometimes manifested in physical symptoms, such as borderline panic attacks with waves of anxiety. John recognises that these symptoms stemmed from Mask-thoughts of being seen, judged, and 'found out'. This became a self-fulfilling prophecy, whereby the Mask's negative thinking and related feelings and behaviours made it difficult for him to perform. At such an event, as the time for him to speak approached, his Mask would whisper thoughts such as: *I am going to muck this up... This isn't going to be good enough... What I've got to say isn't interesting... I don't know what I am talking about... People are going to be judging me on what I say.*

Thankfully, John has quieted his Mask and can now, most of the time, speak in public without the feelings of dread and panic that it used to induce. Over his career, however, he can describe times when his anxiety about public speaking prevented him from taking various opportunities. He knows that he didn't explore avenues of career advancement that were interesting to him at the time because of Mask-thinking. At all costs, John's Mask tried to keep him away from situations where he could be seen, heard, judged, and rejected.

In earlier policy analyst and advocacy positions, John recalls that the roles often required him to present evidence and speak in front of elected officials. He would do anything to avoid this, which often meant other members of his team would step up and get the credit for his work. The restriction John's Mask had placed on him was advancing other people's careers while holding him back.

There are some clear ripple effects of the Mask's control over John in his early leadership journey. For example, even today, when he is proud of something that he has done or achieved, he is reluctant to tell anyone. Like all CEOs, John has to regularly report to the board on his organisation's performance. On one such occasion, John had led the organisation through a successful rebrand that had won an award. Despite the key role he'd played in pushing the rebranding agenda, including deep strategic work that was crucial to its success, he recalls deferring the credit to others, receiving no praise for his important contribution.

Why did John let others take the glory? Yes, that's right – John's Mask was there with its usual tirade of thoughts about him not being worthy of praise or acknowledgement – even though the rebrand was transformative for the organisation. He recalls his Mask suggesting thoughts like: *What I did wasn't important... I didn't add any value... Don't take any credit for that, I didn't do any of it... I could have done more but I didn't, I was lazy.*

Because he deflected praise to others, John began to feel disenfranchised due to the lack of acknowledgement he received. He resigned his position shortly after. In recounting this story, John sees the role his Mask played in creating the situation, including the breakdown in his relationship with the board and, ultimately, his exit from the organisation. He recalls how his Mask's voice changed from beating him up for not being good enough, to isolating him from the board, with thoughts such as: *I don't need their help... It doesn't matter what they think... Who cares anyway?*

With these ideas ringing in his head, it's no wonder he resigned.

This example shows the Mask at its most insidious. In this story, John's Mask-generated thoughts of worthlessness prevented him from taking any praise for his hard work, praise that he deserved. The Mask then reared its ugly head again to offer thoughts of being overlooked and undervalued. For John, this led to him feeling disenfranchised, resulting in the action of him leaving his position. What should have been a hugely proud moment for him was twisted by his Mask into the breakdown of a hitherto strong professional relationship with his board and the ultimate loss of his position.

John's Mask's game plan is clear and has shown up repeatedly on his leadership journey. His Mask is fearful of rejection, linked to his perceived rejection by his mother and father early in his development. Thoughts associated with being rejected include a sense of not being good enough and of being 'found out'. His Mask's perverse strategy, therefore, is to withdraw and opt out before any rejection can take place. *I'll reject them before they reject me*, is its thinking.

If we return to Castillo's model, to get the result of opting out and withdrawing, the Mask assumes an identity that results in the perpetuation of thoughts and feelings that John would never have consciously chosen for himself. John's Mask seems to lean more towards the flight response in the Triple-F system, which manifests his opting-out and withdrawing behaviours.

John's Unmasking Plan

Step 1: Realise

By exposing John's Mask through understanding when it first emerged and by applying Castillo's model, we reveal John's Mask to be fearful of rejection and, relatedly, failure (as this will lead to rejection).

John can gain consciousness by realising when the following thoughts, feelings, and actions appear in his life:

Mask Thoughts	• I'm not good enough
	• I have nothing to say
	• I'm so stupid
	• I should know this
	• I have failed somewhere
	• I am going to get found out
	• I am going to muck this up
	• This isn't going to be good enough
Mask Feelings	• Worthlessness
	• Anxiety
	• Dread
	• Panic
	• Defiance, 'Screw you'
Mask Actions	• Withdrawing
	• Opting out

Step 2: Reject

As soon as John notices any Mask-related thoughts, feelings, and actions, he is conscious. He now must reject what the Mask is offering him.

He can do this by:

1. Finding a private space to focus his energy on increasing his consciousness.

2. Turning attention away from the Mask and towards his breathing to regain control and composure.

3. Discrediting the witness using facts such as:

   - I can't possibly know everything about anything. No one can.

   - I have a Masters-level qualification and rank highly academically.

   - I always do my best.

   - I am the CEO and have risen to this position because I am highly competent.

   - You represent fear. I am not afraid.

Step 3: Respond

With increased consciousness and the Mask now quelled, it is time for John to respond. To counter his Mask, he could choose the following thoughts, feelings, and actions:

Conscious Thoughts	
	• I am enough
	• I have plenty to say
	• I am smart
	• I know this
	• I am successful
	• I am a competent CEO
	• This is going to be a success

(cont.)

Conscious Feelings	• Self-worth
	• Calm
	• Optimism
	• Peace
	• Harmony
Conscious Actions	• Getting involved
	• Opting in

Summary

CEO John first became aware of his Mask at primary school, around the time his father left the family home to be with another woman. John's experience of rejection at a young age meant his Mask learned to fear it, leading to him withdrawing from friendships and from school, leaving with virtually no qualifications.

In his leadership, the Mask kept him fearful of rejection and failure, leading him to avoid situations where he might feel judged or be identified as not knowing what he was talking about. As a result, he avoided public speaking and passed these opportunities to colleagues, who then received praise for his work.

John's Mask places doubts in his head about not knowing enough, along with fears of failing and being 'found out'. John's Unmasking Plan exposes his Mask's typical thoughts, feelings, and actions. Through consciously choosing thoughts such as: *I am enough... I am smart... I know this... I am successful,* John can beat his Mask and access feelings of self-worth, calm, and peace.

EIGHT

The Accountancy Firm Leader

The second case study we're going to look at is that of Laura, the Managing Partner of a large national accountancy firm. With hundreds of staff, the firm has doubled its turnover under her tenure to over £40 million. Confident and outgoing, Laura is a career accountant with over thirty years' experience in the sector.

Exposing the Mask: Laura's story

We begin Laura's story in primary school. Laura tells me she was exceptionally clever, a gifted student. She attended a state-funded school where being academically talented made her vulnerable to bullies. Having been through the Scottish state-school system at the same time as Laura, I can confirm the need for clever students to be wary of being overtly smart. Yet Laura tells me she didn't hide her intellect and her appetite and capacity for knowledge from her peers. Indeed, she did the opposite. Her mantra became: 'I'll show them.'

Being top of the class was a badge of honour for Laura. She was also good at sports, which she believes helped enormously with fending off potential bullies. While the bullies targeted the clever students, Laura noticed they seemed to leave her alone because of her prowess on the sports field. It's interesting how bullies tend to abhor anyone who excels intellectually but are comfortable around those who excel in athletic fields.

At school, Laura appears to have struck an ideal balance. She was comfortable to shine academically, with her above average performance on the sports field keeping the bullies at bay. Laura agrees, reflecting that she was a happy and confident child.

The first time Laura remembers having Mask-thoughts was after she failed a first aid course. While able to acknowledge the triviality of this as an adult, Laura describes it as being one of the most traumatic things she experienced in early childhood. She tells me her Mask at the time sounded like this: *Any idiot could do this... I didn't even have to take this test and I failed it.* Her confidence was severely knocked. With Laura's reputation for being clever, her classmates wasted no time in teasing her for failing such a 'simple' test. Laura recalls feeling incredibly upset by this.

In our mission to expose Laura's Mask, this event appears significant. Following the failure of the first aid test, any other perceived failure, whether that was not getting 100% in an exam, or struggling with a maths challenge, would cause Laura to feel fragile. As adults, it's easy to rationalise that dropping a few points in an exam, or failing a first aid test, doesn't mean you are not clever; that it is not something to be ashamed of. For Laura's young mind, however, these minor failures were tarnishing her identity as 'the clever one' in the family and the classroom and a trigger for Laura's Mask-thinking was born. She recalls thoughts like, *I'm not as good as I think I am... I'm incompetent... This is the start of a slippery slope... What if it all falls apart?*

This Mask-thinking amplified with Laura's transition to secondary school. She describes feeling like she was 'top of the heap' at primary school, but with the move to secondary school, she felt she was at the bottom again. This caused a confidence blip. Being top of the class had become an important part of Laura's identity. Now, surrounded by many other clever pupils, she recalls an internal tension. On one hand, she began thinking that being a top pupil wasn't all that important; on the other, she craved the top spot more than anything else.

Laura accepts that this tension was internal. Her parents were not pushy; they didn't put any pressure on her to over-perform at school. Interestingly, though, Laura recalls her mother often speaking about being top of the class when she was at school. I suspect Laura's Mask might have taken this onboard.

Unscathed by bullying at primary school, Laura now drew the unwelcome attention of bullies at secondary school. She describes herself as skinny, with uncontrollable curly hair, glasses, and a bit of a geek. She had a strong friendship group of similar, like-minded individuals but was wary of the 'cool kids', actively keeping her distance from them. In her experience, these kids would bring her down, commenting on how she looked and what she was wearing. Laura describes these encounters as 'quite scarring'. During face-offs with bullies, Laura describes feeling anger, but trying to keep it all in. She recalls that her Mask would encourage her to attack the bullies, to get them back. While she remained restrained, Laura was aware of her Mask telling her, *I might not do it now, but I'll get them eventually... I will have my revenge.*

As she neared the end of her time at school, Laura felt that she had risen back to the top. As she describes the pleasure she took from engaging with various school activities, it's clear that she was developing into a young leader and was once more comfortable in her own skin. Laura looks back on those final years of secondary school more fondly than the earlier years.

Another transition approached, though, as upon starting university, Laura once again found herself at the bottom of the pile, in an even bigger student pool from which she needed to claw her way back to the top.

Laura's Mask identity

As we did with John, we'll now apply Castillo's model to the emergence of Laura's Mask.

Circumstances: The 'golden child' of the family, who excelled academically and at sports. Laura was often top of the class and enjoyed showing off academically to her classmates. Failure of a first aid test and the transition from primary to secondary school were challenging times for Laura. At secondary school, Laura experienced bullying for the first time.

Thoughts: These circumstances produced Mask-thinking, such as: *Any idiot could have passed this test, but I failed... I'm not as good as I think I am... I'm incompetent... This is the start of a slippery slope... What if it all falls apart?* In relation to those who bullied her, the Mask offered thoughts like, *I might not get them back now, but I'll do it eventually... I will have my revenge.*

Feelings: This Mask-thinking eroded Laura's self-confidence for a time and created a fear of a fall from grace. The feelings that emerged in response to the bullying included anger.

Behaviours/actions: Laura experienced some internalised anger towards her playground tormentors and some withdrawal as she avoided the 'cool' kids at school.

Results: As a result of the above, Laura experienced a short-lived lack of academic confidence.

Impact of Laura's Mask

As an adult, Laura tells me that the Mask's tone hasn't changed much from when she was younger. It sounds strategic and calculating, plotting its revenge against those it perceives to have wronged her. Her Mask had previously offered her thoughts of revenge against school bullies; asked whether her Mask's style is fight, flight, or freeze, she replies, 'Definitely fight.'

While Laura considers herself to be someone who can easily let things go, her Mask is more inclined to hold a grudge. Equally, Laura explains she is the type of person who is quick to apologise if she does something wrong. However, if someone else should point a mistake out to her, she doesn't always receive it well. Such scenarios trigger Laura's Mask, which perceives an adversary that must be seen off. Other triggers for Laura's Mask include being out of the loop, or being overlooked, with her Mask thinking: *What have I done to upset people? Why haven't they invited me? Oh God, what have I done? What have I said?* This leads to feelings of guilt.

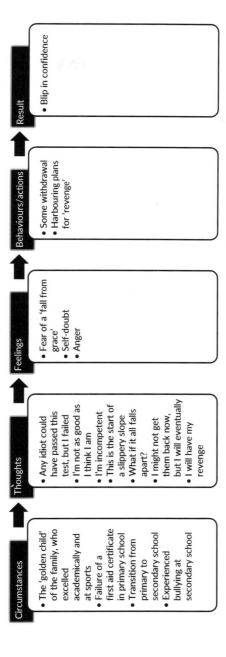

Circumstances

- The 'golden child' of the family, who excelled academically and at sports
- Failure of a first aid certificate in primary school
- Transition from primary to secondary school
- Experienced bullying at secondary school

Thoughts

- Any idiot could have passed this test, but I failed
- I'm not as good as I think I am
- I'm incompetent
- This is the start of a slippery slope
- What if it all falls apart?
- I might not get them back now, but I will eventually have my revenge

Feelings

- Fear of a 'fall from grace'
- Self-doubt
- Anger

Behaviours/actions

- Some withdrawal
- Harbouring plans for 'revenge'

Result

- Blip in confidence

Exposing Laura's Mask

As our conversation flows, Laura reveals she can be mischievous, someone who likes to stir the pot. She explains that sometimes in social situations with friends, and even at board meetings, she may say things that are sailing close to the wind. I ask her to give me an example from the boardroom. To prepare for the monthly board meeting, Laura will review the agenda and often mull over whether she should voice certain issues that she knows will be controversial. Of the examples she gives, some appear strategic, properly thought through, with the pros and cons carefully weighed up. These examples show a Managing Partner consciously calculating risk and reward in their decision making. Yet with other examples, something different is going on. Laura explains that sometimes she has said things at board meetings that really didn't need to be said, almost as a show of strength. This behaviour appears to be less about balancing risk and reward and more about puffing up her chest to show who is in charge, by provoking people.

This Mask-behaviour pattern appears in social situations, too. In friendship groups, there are often things that go unsaid – sometimes, for good reason. Laura recognises she is always the person in her group who voices what other people are thinking. This doesn't always mean the Mask is in control. There can be valid reasons for saying what no one else has the courage to confront. People sometimes do it for fun, playfully, or to hold people to account. But when your words hurt people, including you, it's a sign your Mask is in control. Laura recognises this as we talk through some of her examples. Over the years, Laura has moderated her behaviour and actions, a sign of her increasing consciousness.

Laura is a confident person, whom I have known for many years. Her confidence flows from various positive characteristics and when she thinks, feels, and acts confidently, she mostly does so consciously and to great effect. This is to be celebrated. However, Laura's Mask occasionally hijacks her confidence, tipping it more towards arrogance. When her Mask feels threatened, its tendency is to offer Laura thoughts, feelings, and actions that prepare her for a fight. In her case, a war of words.

Laura's Unmasking Plan

Step 1: Realise

By exposing Laura's Mask through understanding when it first emerged in her early life and applying Castillo's model, we reveal Laura's Mask to be fearful of failure and a 'fall from grace'.

Laura can gain consciousness by realising when the following thoughts, feelings, and actions appear in her life:

Mask Thoughts	
	• I'm not as good as I think I am
	• This is the start of a slippery slope
	• I am incompetent
	• It is all going to fall apart

(Continued)

(cont.)

	•	I will have my revenge
	•	I'll show them
Mask Feelings	•	Diminished confidence
	•	Guilt
Mask Actions	•	Being outspoken and knowing it will cause harm
	•	Plotting 'revenge'

Step 2: Reject

As soon as Laura notices any Mask-related thoughts, feelings, and actions, she is conscious. She now must reject what the Mask is offering her.

She can do this by:

1. Finding a private space to focus her energy on increasing her consciousness.
2. Turning attention away from the Mask and focusing her energy on her breathing to regain control and composure.
3. Discrediting the witness using facts, such as:
   - I am a confident and capable person.
   - I am not afraid of other people's talents.
   - I have been successful throughout my life and will continue to be.
   - I forgive people.

Step 3: Respond

With increased consciousness and the Mask now quelled, it is time for Laura to respond. To counter her Mask, the following thoughts, feelings, and actions are appropriate:

(cont.)

Conscious Thoughts	• I always do my best • I am ambitious • I am intelligent and smart • I forgive people
Conscious Feelings	• Confident • At ease
Conscious Actions	• Being careful with words • Showing empathy

Summary

Laura, the Managing Partner of a national firm of accountants, first became aware of her Mask in primary school. Her Mask appears fearful of failure, of a 'fall from grace'. Academically gifted, Laura's Mask appears to pit her against her peers in an imagined race to the top of the class, with failure to do so resulting in feelings of incompetence, affecting her usually high confidence.

In leadership, Laura's Mask can be confrontational at times, leading her to act in ways that may hurt her and others, including friends. To support her in beating her Mask, Laura can choose thoughts such as: *I am ambitious... I am intelligent and smart... I forgive people... I always do my best.*

NINE

The Wholesale Distribution Leader

Our third case study is of David, the Managing Director of a large fruit and vegetable wholesale distribution business. He is responsible for sixty staff and his company is the largest business of its kind in the local area. Although not a shareholder of this business, David's family has been in the fruit and vegetable sector for over 100 years. Throughout David's childhood, his father ran the business, deciding in 2011 to sell to a large national firm with multiple branches across the UK.

Exposing the Mask: David's story

I asked David to think about the first time in his life he noticed any negative thoughts that his Mask may have offered him. His clearest early memory of the

Mask was around the time his father sold the family business, when David was eighteen and a driver for the company. He recalls how, after the sale, more people became involved in the business and it went from a small, family-run operation to a larger concern with national links.

On some level, David worried about where his future might lie now that his father had sold the business. He recalls thinking: *I'll just stay a driver because, in a big company like this, there is little chance for me. I will just stay where I am.* David is clear that he would not consciously choose to think this way today and feels this is an example of how his Mask used to control his life.

I encouraged David to go deeper and think of an earlier time when he recognised the Mask in his life. At fifteen, David displayed some behaviours that he now recognises as Mask-related. David paints a picture of a younger, more arrogant version of himself, buoyed by his family's successful business, with his family name 'above the door'. He had a comfortable life and admitted that he perhaps didn't appreciate the value of what his family had worked hard to provide. To illustrate, David spoke of his PlayStation games console – a relatively costly item for most families. His attitude at the time meant he didn't look after such items with the care they deserved; he knew that, if he needed a new console, his family would provide it for him. Hard as it is for David to admit, he knows that this attitude was a consistent theme for him in his early teens. He recalls his school friends commenting on his family's wealth, including their big house, their expensive cars, and the frequent holidays they would go on. His attitude back then was one of conceit. He revelled in the attention it brought him from his friends, who admired his family's wealth and status.

As he looks back on his behaviour, David now realises how much control his Mask had in his life at that time. He recalls how his Mask would encourage him to be 'cocky', to act disrespectfully, and to 'take things for granted'. His Mask would offer him thoughts like: *It doesn't matter because whatever happens, I come from money, so it will be fine... No matter what I do, there will always be a way out for me.*

As he progressed through his teenage years, the Mask's voice amplified. At its worst, David recalls how he would show off to his friends about his new car that he wasn't even old enough to drive yet. It quite embarrassed David to reflect on how he must have appeared to those who knew him back then: 'I had a complete lack of awareness about how I must have come across to people. Yet, in that moment, I thought everything was cool. I was the man.'

As David and I continued to discuss his Mask, its typical thoughts, feelings, and behaviours, to better understand its identity, we unearthed that his Mask wanted him to be a people pleaser, so that he would fit in and be a 'part of the cool gang'.

This led me to ask whether David had ever experienced a time when he didn't fit in. Is this what his Mask was fearful of? This line of questioning took David immediately back to primary school. He recalls with utter clarity often being the last boy to be picked for football. He tells me, 'It was literally like the way it was in the movies. I would be the last person standing, the guy none of the teams wanted.' David recalls that his Mask, in this situation, would say to him: *I am not good enough... No one wants me.*

This pattern of Mask-thinking continued throughout primary school until it came time to plan for the transition to secondary school. David's parents offered him the opportunity to go to a private secondary school, together with most of his primary school mates. Yet David refused, opting instead to attend the local comprehensive school where few of his peers would go. As the time to start secondary school drew near, David remembers his Mask offering thoughts, such as: *I've had it... I am in for a rough ride.* His Mask now switched to generating fear about what might lie ahead for him at secondary school.

David cannot explain why he decided not to attend the private school that most of his school friends would be going to but, after some reflection, says he can remember regretting it even before he started at his new secondary school. He recalls feeling panicked about the decision and frustration at not understanding why he'd rejected the offer of private schooling.

I asked David if he could recall a time when the Mask-thoughts of *No one wants me* might have occurred at home, and he explained that his relationship with his father, particularly when he was around six years old, left him feeling like he was an inconvenience. David remembers doing his utmost to get his father's attention and approval from a young age, but consistently feeling like a burden. He told me about a day when he was at home with only his father and had the idea of doing something fun together, just the two of them. David suggested they both go on a walk. His idea was met with an abrupt, 'No.' What he found especially memorable was how emphatically his father delivered this response, leaving David feeling stupid for having even asked.

David's experiences of rejection by his father appear to have triggered his Mask. At school, his classmates amplified this when they didn't pick him for the football team. By the time he was getting ready to leave for secondary school, David's Mask had filled his head with thoughts of not being good enough and not being wanted. Having exposed his Mask during our interview, it seemed that perhaps the decision about where to attend secondary school was a tipping point in David's development, the point at which Mask-thoughts became Mask-behaviours.

David's Mask, in its perverse attempt to 'protect' him from rejection, may have offered as a solution the thought of going to a school where he didn't know anyone. This decision may also have been a message to his father, whom he blamed for rejecting him as a child. The rationale behind David's decision is unclear. But the question of *who* decided is clear – to me, at least. Given that David immediately regretted the decision and recalls it causing him physical anxiety – remember, thoughts, feelings, and actions that you wouldn't choose for yourself are a sign that your Mask is in control – I surmise that his Mask made this decision for him. Having made this crucial decision for him, the insidious Mask now filled David's head with fear about the rough time he was going to have at his new school.

David's Mask identity

Again, applying Castillo's model to the emergence of David's Mask helps to expose its identity.

Circumstances: David's father ran a successful family fruit and veg business, which had provided the family with great wealth. At school, David was often picked last for team sports. At home, he struggled to get his father's attention.

Thoughts: These circumstances produced Mask-thoughts, such as: *It doesn't matter because whatever happens, I come from money, so it will be fine... No matter what I do, there will always be a way out for me... I'm not good enough... No one wants me.*

Feelings: This Mask-thinking made David feel like an inconvenience and unwanted by his father. At school, he felt like he wasn't good enough, even worthless. In relation to his family's material wealth, he felt conceit.

Behaviours/actions: To try and feel good enough and to fit in at school, David behaved arrogantly, showing off about his family's wealth in an attempt to get closer to the 'cool kids'. He chose not to attend a private secondary school, perhaps to reject those schoolmates who had rejected him. While working in his father's business, his conceitedness translated into laziness.

Results: As a result of his Mask-thinking, David missed out on the opportunity to experience a private education. Hanging out with the 'cool kids' led to him engaging in anti-social behaviour, with some police involvement, and not applying himself at work; as a result, David's father fired him from the family business.

Impact of David's Mask

It is difficult to estimate the impact of David's decision to pass up on the opportunity to get a private education on his life chances. Certainly, in his case, the environment of the local comprehensive school he ultimately attended was less conducive to learning and growth. A clearer impact is evident in the outlet

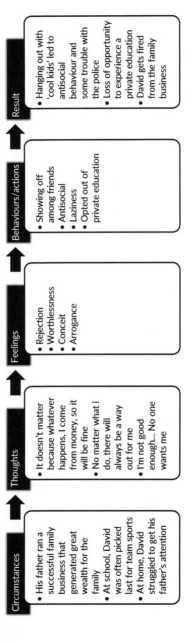

Circumstances
- His father ran a successful family business that generated great wealth for the family
- At school, David was often picked last for team sports
- At home, David struggled to get his father's attention

Thoughts
- It doesn't matter because whatever happens, I come from money, so it will be fine
- No matter what I do, there will always be a way out for me
- I'm not good enough... No one wants me

Feelings
- Rejection
- Worthlessness
- Conceit
- Arrogance

Behaviours/actions
- Showing off among friends
- Antisocial
- Laziness
- Opted out of private education

Result
- Hanging out with 'cool kids' led to antisocial behaviour and some trouble with the police
- Loss of opportunity to experience a private education
- David gets fired from the family business

Exposing David's Mask

David's Mask-behaviours found in the comprehensive school environment. In its bid to avoid rejection and bring David closer to the 'cool kids', his Mask chose behaviours and actions that were not representative of who he would have chosen to be, including arrogance and showboating.

In the context of David's leadership journey, his Mask's fear of rejection and thoughts of not being good enough placed tremendous pressure on him as he worked his way up the ladder. He recognises that this has often led to him taking on too much work. When asked to do something, David is disinclined to say no because he doesn't want others to think that he can't cope. In his mind, the more he does, the lower the chances of him being rejected. By exceeding people's expectations of him, he increases his chances of fitting in, of being accepted, of becoming an indispensable member of the senior leadership team. This has heaped unnecessary pressure on him, resulting in exhaustion, misdirected focus at work, and a failure to prioritise time at home with his young family.

This pressure and the resulting exhaustion can lead David to be less conscious, giving his Mask an opening. During these infrequent moments, David's normally upbeat personality and 'can do' attitude is eroded and replaced with pessimism and hopelessness.

David's Unmasking Plan

Step 1: Realise

By exposing David's Mask through understanding when it first emerged in his early life and by applying Castillo's model, we reveal David's Mask to be fearful of rejection and of not fitting in.

David can gain consciousness by realising when the following thoughts, feelings, and actions appear in his life:

Mask Thoughts	• I'm not good enough
	• No one wants me
	• I need approval
	• I'm lazy
Mask Feelings	• Unconfident
	• Regret
	• Anxiety
Mask Actions	• Working long hours
	• Prioritising the wrong things
	• Not spending enough quality time at home

Step 2: Reject

As soon as David notices any Mask-related thoughts, feelings, and actions, he is conscious. He now must reject what the Mask is offering him.

(cont.)

He can do this by:

1. Finding a private space to focus his energy on increasing his consciousness.

2. Turning attention away from the Mask and towards his breathing to regain control and composure.

3. Discrediting the witness using facts such as:

   - I have worked hard to prove my worth in my career.

   - I am a respected and capable professional.

   - I am a beloved husband, father, son, friend, and colleague.

Step 3: Respond

With increased consciousness and the Mask now quelled, it is time for David to respond. To counter his Mask, the following thoughts, feelings, and actions are appropriate:

Conscious Thoughts	• I am enough
	• I am loved
	• I am needed
	• I need only my own approval
	• I am hardworking and resourceful
Conscious Feelings	• Confident
	• At peace
	• Calm
Conscious Actions	• Keeping his working hours in check
	• Focusing on the 'right' things
	• Prioritising time at home

Summary

David, the Managing Director of a national fruit and vegetable wholesaler, first noticed his Mask appear in school, associated with feelings of rejection both in the playground and by his father at home. Coming from a wealthy family, David's Mask encouraged him to showboat as a tactic to fit in with the 'cool kids' at school and avoid rejection. His Mask-based arrogance and conceit meant David did not apply himself at school or in the family business, leading to his father firing him.

In his leadership, David is aware that his Mask can push him to overwork and to focus on the wrong things in an attempt to avoid rejection due to failure. There is also an element of seeking acceptance from his superiors, meaning he works long hours and doesn't always get the balance he wants between his personal and professional lives.

David's Unmasking Plan includes consciously choosing thoughts such as: *I am enough... I am loved... I am needed... I need only my own approval.* This kind of conscious thinking will counter the Mask-related feelings of anxiety with feelings of peace and calm.

TEN

The Education Leader

M ark is the principal of a further education college with 500 students and an annual income of £4 million. His leadership career has mainly been in the education sector, with his current position being his first as a principal.

Exposing the Mask: Mark's story

Mark is the youngest child of three. His brother is seven years his senior and his sister, three-and-a-half years older. As a child, Mark looked up to his brother, who was captain of the rugby team, as a hero. His sister was an academic, always acing her exams. In comparison, Mark described himself as 'just good at drama'. Mark suspects this might be where his Mask began comparing him with others.

Mark first recalls actually noticing his Mask while he was in his second year of drama college, aged twenty. His college was going on a drama tour in Canada and students had been invited to audition for various parts, including some leading roles. Mark had often auditioned for significant roles in college and excelled. The tour should have been well within his reach. But despite having the talent, Mark didn't audition. Typical Mask-thinking (*No, I'm not going to audition, I'm not good enough... There are people who are better than me*) got in his way and he passed the opportunity up.

Following the auditions, Mark's drama teacher asked him why he hadn't put himself forward. Mark repeated his Mask-thinking of not being good enough. His teacher replied, 'I had you in my top three, one of the people I was keen to see audition. But you didn't come forward, so there's nothing I can do about it.' He then gave Mark some sage advice, telling him, 'You have to shoot for the moon – even if you miss, even if you hit a lamppost on the way, don't talk yourself down. You should have auditioned.' Mark took this advice to heart and made it his mantra.

Other than this incident, Mark doesn't recall the Mask being present much in his early life. He tells me, 'I've always been quite successful. If I put myself forward for something, I would normally get it.' Three months after landing his first job in education, Mark was offered the role of head of the department. His mantra of 'shoot for the moon' was serving him well, encouraging him to grab opportunities with both hands. This helped him to ignore his Mask, to set it aside and choose consciously for most of his career and life.

Mark's experience with the Mask is common. The Mask can present itself at any time in our lives. For me, it appeared at five and has been a source of constant, often daily torment, for decades. I know many people who have had a similar experience. Equally, a lot of people move happily through life without being aware of their Mask or experiencing any significant negative consequences from it. In Mark's case, despite missing out on what could have been a glorious trip to Canada, he has been a successful educational leader and hasn't been aware of the Mask's influence at all throughout his diverse and interesting career. I feel glad for him that he has enjoyed such freedom from the control of his Mask. But Mark's story doesn't end here because, after thirty years, Mark's Mask is back with a vengeance.

At the time of writing this book, Mark's Mask has re-emerged, intent on convincing him that he doesn't have enough knowledge or experience to be in his current leadership position, that others would be better than him, and that his peers know this. His Mask further undermines his confidence by offering additional thoughts such as: *I'm not brainy enough to come up with solutions... Even if I do come up with a solution, it probably won't work... It wouldn't be as good as other people's ideas.*

Such thinking is often called 'imposter syndrome', but the medical connotations of a term like 'syndrome' make it sound more complex and worrying than it needs to be. I prefer to use the term 'imposter thoughts'. These thoughts are generated by – you guessed it – the Mask. Imposter thoughts feed on the fear of not being good enough, of being 'found out' for imagined failings.

To expose Mark's Mask, to understand its origins and why it offers him such unhelpful, negative thoughts we look back on his life, focusing on his time in college. Mark recalls that he was surrounded by, in his own words, 'talented people who had succeeded and were clearly very good at what they did.' In the present day, Mark knows that when he is in a room with other leaders, his Mask-thinking sounds like: *These are proper leaders... These people know their stuff and I don't... I'd better be quiet in case they find out I don't know what I'm talking about.*

The similarity in Mask-thinking between when Mark was in college and now in his current leadership role, is striking. In both situations, Mark's Mask gets him to think that he is surrounded by people who are the best in their field. Mark tells me that the entry standard for his drama school was high: 'You don't get in if you're rubbish. You've got to be good.' The irony in what he's telling me is not immediately obvious to Mark, so I point it out.

'In the two scenarios you've shared with me, you perceived everyone around you as highly accomplished leaders in their fields. At drama college, you recognised the talent in others, telling me the entry standards were tough and that only the best got in. In your current role as principal of a further education college, the leadership qualities of others intimidate you. You have described feeling sub-standard by comparison.'

Mark appears to be blind to his own accomplishments, while he can easily recognise the same accomplishments in others. When he was at college, such thinking prevented him from auditioning for what could have been the opportunity of a lifetime. In his current leadership role, he worries over certain decisions, fearful that other people's ideas are better than his. In the past eighteen months he has experienced physical symptoms of anxiety, including leg tremors, a racing heart, tinnitus, and panic attacks. It is clear that Mask-thinking is robbing Mark of his confidence and making his job a source of distress. Instead of feeling rightly confident and competent, his Mask is leaving him feeling fearful, inadequate, and like a failure.

We do some fact checking to help Mark reject his Mask. I remind him that he went through the same rigorous entry process as everyone else to get into his drama college, and that they don't let 'rubbish' people in, only the best. 'That included you,' I tell him. 'And I'm sure many excellent candidates applied for the principal role that you are in now. None of those other people who are "better" than you got the job – you did.' I remind Mark, 'When you are experiencing feelings of fear, inadequacy, and failure, you are not in control – your Mask is.' He is silent for a moment, with the full impact that the Mask is having on his leadership sinking in.

Mark's Mask identity

Let's now apply Castillo's model to the emergence of Mark's Mask.

Circumstances: Mark came from a stable home with two older siblings whose talent he admired. After graduating from secondary school, he was accepted to study at a prestigious drama college and had an opportunity to audition for a college trip to Canada.

Thoughts: These circumstances lead to Mask-thoughts such as: *I'm not good enough... There are people who are better than me... I'm not clever enough.*

Feelings: These thoughts generate feelings of self-doubt, with Mark feeling like a fraud, an imposter.

Behaviours/actions: These feelings lead to Mark comparing himself with his peers and finding himself constantly falling short. He decides not to audition for the trip to Canada because he doesn't feel good enough.

Results: Marks misses out on the opportunity to tour Canada, denying himself an exciting life experience.

Impact of Mark's Mask

Mark's leadership journey has taken him all over the world and he has held various positions within the education sector, including head of department and leader of staff, but this is the first time he's been a principal. This makes his current position unfamiliar territory, which triggers his Mask.

From what we know of Mark's Mask identity, it appears to offer him thoughts that he is not good enough. His Mask often compares him with others, and he always falls short. His Mask tells him he is not as experienced, talented, or knowledgeable as his peers and, what's more, they know it. Given that Mark has held other senior roles without his Mask getting in the way, something about this position must be different. After thirty years of silence, what has triggered his Mask?

I ask Mark to describe a recent scenario when his Mask was triggered and what impact that had on him.

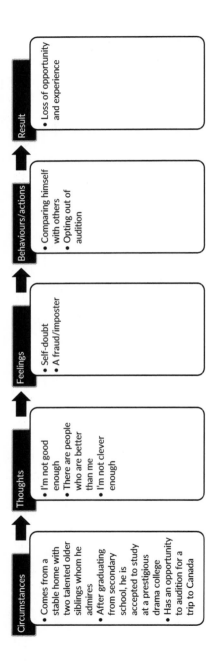

Circumstances	Thoughts	Feelings	Behaviours/actions	Result
• Comes from a stable home with two talented older siblings whom he admires • After graduating from secondary school, he is accepted to study at a prestigious drama college • Has an opportunity to audition for a trip to Canada	• I'm not good enough • There are people who are better than me • I'm not clever enough	• Self-doubt • A fraud/imposter	• Comparing himself with others • Opting out of audition	• Loss of opportunity and experience

Exposing Mark's Mask

Immediately, he tells me about his senior leadership team meetings. When he is chairing these meetings, if his Mask offers him thoughts about the inadequacy of his leadership, he can feel paralysed. In this frozen state, he doesn't feel able to offer solutions, opinions, or ideas in meetings. He can recall several such occasions. What's more, if no one else offers ideas or solutions to agenda items, Mark thinks this is his fault.

Then there are the meetings he has with parents of students. Such meetings are often challenging, with Mark having to manage parents' concerns and expectations sensitively in the context of running a large educational organisation. Recalling a recent meeting in which he was being berated by some parents, he thought: *Crumbs, this is not good. I need to get out of here.*

As well as Mask-thoughts telling him he is not a good leader and anything that goes wrong at the college is his fault, Mark has experienced some physical symptoms. On more than one occasion, he recalls his leg shaking uncontrollably because of the anxiety induced by Mask-thinking. Mark's Mask has taken him from a confident, positive guy to someone who is constantly doubting himself. When his Mask is in control, Mark questions his abilities as a leader, has difficulty making decisions, and feels defeated.

Contrasting his Mask-thinking when he was in his twenties with now, Mark realises the thought of not being good enough compared to others is still present. Thinking back to the start of his tenure as principal, he feels like his leadership team were lost because they weren't sure who he was as a leader, what his beliefs and priorities were. His Mask prevented him from portraying the leader he wanted to be. Mark feels this was because he wasn't being himself. He wasn't showing up as his conscious self; his Mask was showing up instead and, rather than showing who Mark was, as a unique confident leader, his Mask offered what it thought a leader should be. Even Mark's wife was worried, as she didn't recognise him, observing how unusually quiet he was in the evening. The Mask was firmly in control and visible to those who knew him well.

In one of Mark's more conscious moments, he tried to gain perspective on how he was feeling. He asked himself: *Wasn't this supposed to be the best job in the world? Do I not have an amazing opportunity to shape and develop young minds?* Why did he feel miserable? He resolved to take one day at a time, hoping that each day would get better. And it did.

The turning point for Mark was when he took back some control from the Mask and let his unique self shine through. He did this by leaning back into his passion for drama and performing, even singing at a school event. Finally, students, parents, and staff got to see who he was and what mattered to him, in life and in leadership.

I continue to support Mark through my coaching programme. His Mask still shows up and tries to sabotage him. When he has a good day, he might become fearful that bad news is just around the corner. A sign that his Mask is attempting to regain control. It pushes him to leave the present moment and worry about a future that may never happen – his Mask has a PhD in catastrophising – but Mark is winning the internal war.

Mark's Unmasking Plan

Step 1: Realise

By exposing Mark's Mask through understanding when it first emerged in his early life and by applying Castillo's model, we reveal Mark's Mask to be fearful of being found out as a fraud.

Mark can gain consciousness by realising when the following thoughts, feelings, and actions appear in his life:

Mask Thoughts	
	• I'm not good enough
	• Other people are better than me
	• I'm not clever enough
	• My ideas are not as good as other people's
	• I don't know my stuff
	• I am not as a good of a leader as other people

(Continued)

(cont.)

Mask Feelings	•	Imposter
	•	Unconfident
	•	Anxious
	•	Intimidated
	•	Inadequate
	•	Defeated
	•	Deflated
Mask Actions	•	Comparing himself with others
	•	Withdrawing
	•	Freezing when it comes to decision making and idea generation

Step 2: Reject

As soon as Mark notices any Mask-related thoughts, feelings, and actions, he is conscious. He now must reject what the Mask is offering him.

He can do this by:

1. Finding a private space to focus his energy on increasing his consciousness.

2. Turning attention away from the Mask and towards his breathing to regain control and composure.

3. Discrediting the witness using facts such as:

   - I am as successful as the people who surround me.

   - I have had a very successful career.

   - I have been promoted throughout my career.

Step 3: Respond

With increased consciousness and the Mask now quelled, it is time for Mark to respond. To counter his Mask, the following thoughts, feelings, and actions are appropriate:

Conscious Thoughts	• I am enough
	• I will not compare myself with others
	• I am intelligent
	• I have good ideas and suggestions that I will share with others
	• I am knowledgeable
	• I am a confident leader
Conscious Feelings	• Authentic
	• Confident
	• Calm
	• Brave
	• Abundant
	• Victorious
	• Pumped-up
Conscious Actions	• Never comparing himself with others
	• Opting in
	• Being open to sharing ideas and suggestions
	• Being confident in decision making

Summary

Mark, the principal of a large college, first noticed his Mask appear in his early twenties while at drama school. His Mask compares him with his peers, usually finding Mark inadequate in some way. As a result of such thinking, he turns down an opportunity to audition for a role he was likely to have been awarded.

In his leadership, Mark's Mask has been dormant until his recent appointment as principal, upon which it has returned with gusto. Its familiar pattern of comparing him (unfavourably) with his peers has resulted in Mark feeling that his leadership skills and qualities are inferior. This has significantly affected Mark's confidence and enjoyment of his new role.

To counter Mark's Mask-thinking, he must be aware of when he is comparing himself with others, a sure sign that his Mask is in control. Additionally, conscious thoughts such as: *I have good ideas and suggestions... I am a confident leader... I am knowledgeable... I am enough*, will help him to feel authentic, confident, calm, and brave.

ELEVEN

The Brand Management Leader

Angela is the CEO and sole shareholder of a small brand management company. Over ten years, Angela has built her company to a team of twenty staff with revenue of £2 million per year. Her business is in a good place, having weathered the Covid-19 storm, and looking to grow over the next three to five years.

Exposing the Mask: Angela's story

Angela first recalls having Mask-thoughts at secondary school, at age fourteen. She remembers this as a lonely time in her life where she felt low, sad, and had little confidence. Angela didn't like her school and struggled to be happy. She'd had a positive experience at primary school, but found the transition to secondary difficult.

As Angela and I talk, we identify a couple of factors that may have contributed to the growing sense of isolation she felt. Primary school had been a happy time for her, with her firm friendships being a source of great joy. Unfortunately, when she transitioned to secondary school, she was not put in the same classes as her primary school friends. Describing some pupils in her new classes as 'badly behaved', Angela found it hard to make new connections. She didn't feel like she fitted in. This was the first time in her life Angela recalls feeling anxiety. Another factor we identify from this time was the appearance of facial acne. Despite seeking medical advice and receiving treatment, nothing seemed to help. This pulled Angela's mood and confidence down yet further.

The feeling of anxiety affected her interactions at school, where she was reluctant to speak up in the classroom or in groups with friends. She also quickly lost interest in school activities, signing up but then dropping out shortly afterwards. Angela sums up her feelings then as being 'down in the dumps, I really didn't have a lot of confidence.' Angela can recall how she felt at this point in her life without hesitation, but when asked if she can remember the associated thoughts, she struggles.

At home, Angela lived with her mum, dad, and an older brother; she tells me she had a 'reasonably happy' childhood. When Angela was nine, her father had a heart attack, from which he didn't make a full recovery, trying but ultimately unable to re-enter the workforce. Angela describes her mother as 'quite volatile' with frequent mood swings. She tells me, 'You never really knew how you were going to get her. She could go into a bad mood for weeks at a time and not really speak to us. I tried to keep my distance from her.' I ask Angela if she was aware of her Mask during these episodes. Again, she cannot recall what, if any, negative thoughts she may have had, but remembers feeling unhappy at home at these times – she was sad for her mother. Angela left home at nineteen. She explains that her mother and father were happy together, but that they were not happy people. Angela remembers wanting to 'escape' the family home, feeling that it was not a happy environment.

This revelation gives us some insight that helps expose Angela's Mask. In telling her story of leaving home, she uses language such as 'escaping negativity'. Angela's mother's extreme mood swings must have been hard for her to comprehend at such a young age; perhaps this is what first triggered her Mask, which now perceives negativity as a threat, something that she must escape from.

Angela's Mask identity

Let's now apply Castillo's model to the emergence of Angela's Mask.

Circumstances: Angela lived at home with her mother, father, and older brother. Angela's father suffered a heart attack and could no longer work. Her mother experienced mood swings for weeks at a time. The transition to secondary school was challenging for Angela and she developed facial acne during puberty, which did not respond to treatment.

Thoughts: Angela cannot recall what thoughts her Mask offered her during this time in her life; she recalls only the feelings.

Feelings: Angela remembers feeling a lack of confidence, with low mood. At school, she didn't feel she fitted in and was anxious. At home, she felt trapped.

Behaviours/actions: Angela was reluctant to speak up in the classroom or when in groups with other pupils. She lost interested in school activities, often dropping out of things she'd expressed interest in. At home, she avoided her mother. Overall, Angela became withdrawn.

Results: Angela left home at nineteen to escape the 'negative' environment.

Impact of Angela's Mask

Today, as a successful entrepreneur, Angela is relatively free from her Mask, but she knows it can still sometimes impact her leadership and life. The most

Circumstances	Thoughts	Feelings	Behaviours/actions	Result
• Lived at home with her mother, father and older brother • Angela's father suffered a heart attack and could no longer work • Her mother experienced mood swings for weeks at a time • The transition to secondary school was challenging for Angela • She developed facial acne during puberty that did not respond to treatment	• Angela was unable to identify any thoughts	• Low mood • Insecure • Anxious • Trapped	• Not speaking up in the classroom or in groups of other pupils • Dropping out of school activites • Avoidance of her mother • Withdrawal	• Left home at nineteen to escape the 'negative' environment

Exposing Angela's Mask

common form of Mask-thinking affecting her today is worrying about things that might never happen, and the associated panic and fear that results from visualising such events.

Angela tells me that this can happen on quite a small scale. For example, she regularly plays tennis with a group of friends. One weekend, her friends invited some new people she didn't know to join them for a match. This triggered her Mask, which generated a feeling of anxiety and offered her thoughts like, *I'm playing tennis in front of these new people, so I'd better play well.*

Angela recognises that her Mask often offers her things to worry about, in her business and in her life. A keen gym-goer, Angela has had the same personal trainer for five years. Even after all that time, Angela gets anxious ahead of every training session. It is hard for Angela to rationalise, but she describes it as an internal monologue in which her Mask says: *I have agreed to do this personal training session, so I'd better get it done, and it's going to be tough.* This continues until the moment she arrives at the gym. The Mask myopically focuses on the commitment Angela has made and creates a feeling of being under pressure.

As we continue to talk, it becomes clear that Angela's Mask repeats this same pattern with all the various innocuous appointments and commitments she might make in a typical week. She tells me how, when taking her children to the cinema at the weekend, her Mask would say things like: *I need to get to the cinema on time... This is quite a long movie – is it too long?* Rather than enjoying the movie she has consciously taken her children to see, her Mask has her incessantly worrying.

In this example, the fear of not being able to escape resurfaces. Angela explained that when she goes to a theatre or cinema, she must always be close to the aisle. She cannot sit in the middle of a row. Reflecting on her time at university, when she would attend lectures in large auditoriums, Angela said that the fear of not being able to escape and this bringing on a panic attack was acute.

The need to escape was first mentioned by Angela in the context of leaving her negative home environment. In our conversation, Angela also mentions a member of her team who she feels is 'rather negative'. During an exchange with this team member, Angela recalls wanting to 'escape' the office to get away from this person. I dislike negativity as much as the next person and I can certainly emphasise with not wanting to hang around an overly negative person for longer than is necessary. I might think twice about meeting such a friend for coffee, or bring someone else along to lift the mood. But external negativity doesn't trigger my Mask. I make a conscious decision to avoid it. In Angela's case, and perhaps because of the context in which she grew up, external negativity triggers her Mask. For her, it brings to the surface feelings of anxiety and an associated need to escape, to take flight.

Angela's Unmasking Plan

Step 1: Realise

By exposing Angela's Mask through understanding when it first emerged in her early life and by applying Castillo's model, we reveal it to be fearful of negativity and of not being able to escape.

Angela can gain consciousness by realising when the following thoughts, feelings, and actions appear in her life:

Mask Thoughts	Angela cannot identify what thoughts her Mask offers her, only the feelings.
Mask Feelings	• Sad • Lonely • Unconfident • Isolated • Anxious • Trapped • Worried
Mask Actions	• Withdrawing • Being reluctant to speak • Trying to escape • Failure to be in the moment

Step 2: Reject

As soon as Angela notices any Mask-related thoughts, feelings, and actions, she is conscious. She now must reject what the Mask is offering her.

She can do this by:

1. Finding a private space to focus her energy on increasing her consciousness.

2. Turning attention away from the Mask and towards her breathing to regain control and composure.

3. Discrediting the witness using facts such as:

   - Throughout my career and life, I have coped with any issues I have faced.

   - Yes, I have made a commitment to personal training. I do this routinely and don't need to worry about it. This is not something I have to worry about.

Step 3: Respond

With increased consciousness and the Mask now quelled, it is time for Angela to respond. To counter her Mask, the following thoughts, feelings, and actions are appropriate:

Conscious Thoughts	• I am present in the now
	• I am confident
	• I am capable
	• There is nothing to fear and nothing to escape from

(Continued)

(cont.)

Conscious Feelings	•	Happy
	•	Confident
	•	Calm
	•	Free
	•	Peaceful
Conscious Actions	•	Focusing on the now, not an imagined future

Summary

Angela owns a successful branding company. She struggles to recall the thoughts her Mask offers her but can recognise how it makes her feel and act. She first became aware of the Mask at school, where it was associated with a complete crash in confidence. Angela perceived her home environment to be extremely negative; she felt trapped there and wanted to escape.

In her leadership and life, Angela's Mask is a worrier. It makes her worry about innocuous things, such as meeting new people, doing activities with her children, and attending the gym. Mimicking feelings of being trapped in her home life, Angela seeks to escape negative situations at work.

To support Angela, conscious thoughts such as: *I am present in the now... I am confident... My commitments are nothing to worry about*, will help her to spend more time in the present moment and less time in the psychological fear offered to her by the Mask.

Final Thoughts

I am aware that this is not your typical leadership or business book. It contains a lot of sensitive content and vulnerability that might be uncomfortable for many people to read.

In writing the book, my Mask was a constant companion, telling me not to write it, not to share the highly personal story that I have laid bare. Perhaps the five CEOs I interviewed had similar Mask-thoughts. I chose to ignore these thoughts and write this book because too few people are openly sharing their stories and talking about the impact their inner negative voice is having on their leadership and lives.

There is plenty of content out there on imposter syndrome and how it can affect leaders, yet such articles never seem to expose the human side of this very real issue. We all have personal histories that have affected us in some way. Given we have this in common, why are we so reluctant to open up?

The answer of course, is the Mask. Any resistance you have felt while reading this book has come from your Mask. From its fear of being found out, of you rediscovering and reclaiming your identity and ultimately rejecting the Mask.

I don't want to live in fear anymore. That's why I have written this book and shared it with you. The destructive impact my own Mask had on my life has been the strongest motivator. For if the Mask could so effectively assume my identity and rule my life with fear, then there must be others like me. My leadership coaching has reinforced this view. I haven't yet had a client who has not been impacted by the Mask.

The need for us to become more conscious is the greatest priority facing humanity today. I thank Richard and Liz for waking me up. I want this book to be *your* alarm call. It's time for you to wake up and regain control of your leadership, life, and confidence.

Further Reading

Assaraf, J, *Innercise: The new science to unlock your brain's hidden power* (Waterside Productions, 2018)

Brown, D, *Happy: Why more or less everything is absolutely fine* (Penguin, 2018)

Chopra, D, *The Higher Self: The magic of inner and outer fulfilment* (Nightingale-Conant, 2014)

Chopra, D, *Metahuman: Unleashing your infinite potential* (Penguin, 2019)

Covey, SR, *The 7 Habits of Highly Effective People* (Simon and Schuster, 2003)

Cuddy, A, *Presence: Bringing your boldest self to your biggest challenges* (Orion Publishing Group, 2015)

Dispenza, J, *Breaking the Habit of Being Yourself: How to lose your mind and create a new one* (Encephalon, 2020)

Hawkins, J, *A Thousand Brains: A new theory of intelligence* (Basic Books, 2021)

Lencioni, PM, *The Five Dysfunctions of a Team: A leadership fable* (Random House Publishing, 2002)

Mate, G, *When the Body Says No: The cost of hidden stress* (Penguin, 2021)

Peters, S, *The Chimp Paradox: The mind management programme for confidence, success and happiness* (Random House, 2012)

Peterson, JB, *12 Rules for Life: An antidote to chaos* (Penguin, 2018)

Pink, DH, *The Power of Regret: How looking backward moves us forward* (Canongate Books, 2022)

Stevens, A, *Jung: A very short introduction* (Oxford University Press, 2001)(Naxos, 2004)

Tolle, E, *The Power of Now: A guide to spiritual enlightenment* (New World Library, 2000)

Acknowledgements

This book would not have been possible without the love, guidance, and support of Richard Wilkins and Liz Ivory, my mentors. Thanks to you both for showing me how to choose and waking me up to a new reality, freer from the demons of my past. You have helped countless people rediscover who they are, and you continue to be an inspiration for so many. Keep shining your light.

To my mum, Jackie, and sister, Claire, thanks for standing by my side, for supporting me throughout my life, and for believing in me as I started the journey of writing this book. I know it must have been hard for you to read parts of my story. Your love is such a powerful source of strength.

To the leaders who graciously gave their time to be interviewed for this book, and who trusted me enough to be vulnerable and share their story, thank you.

I am immensely grateful to my colleagues at Vistage International (UK), particularly Laura Gordon and Graeme Thompson, who believed in me enough to support my mission in sharing the important messages of this book.

To all my amazing friends, thank you for being in my life. I especially want to thank Angela Clarke and Angela Bolton; you are my oldest friends and know me better than most.

Finally, I would like to acknowledge Action on Asbestos for their dedicated work in raising awareness of mesothelioma, a rare form of cancer linked to asbestos exposure. They tirelessly advocate on behalf of those affected and provide much-needed support.

The Author

Gavin Bryce is the founder of Constant Progression Limited, a boutique leadership coaching and management consultancy, based in the UK. He has over twenty-five years' global experience in the private, public, and not-for-profit sectors. Gavin founded his first business in 2007, building a multimillion-pound portfolio in the areas of health and international development. Now focused on coaching and supporting leaders of small- and medium-sized businesses, Gavin's purpose is to magnify the potential of others to live fulfilling and impactful lives. This is his first book on a topic that is a passion for him. His own experience of battling with, and overcoming, the negative inner voice motivates him to help others struggling with their inner saboteur. Based in Scotland, Gavin offers his services worldwide to those leaders and their teams who want to rediscover their inner confidence and to work and communicate more effectively.

🌐 www.constantprogression.uk

in www.linkedin.com/in/gavintbryce